# Exploring the Python Library Ecosystem: A Comprehensive Guide

Kameron Hussain and Frahaan Hussain

Published by Sonar Publishing, 2023.

EXPLORING THE PYTHON LIBRARY ECOSYSTEM: A COMPREHENSIVE GUIDE

**First edition. November 9, 2023.**



ISBN: 979-8223267058

Written by Kameron Hussain and Frahaan Hussain.

# Table of Contents


Chapter 1: Introduction to Python Libraries

Section 1.1: What Are Python Libraries?

Benefits of Python Libraries

Common Python Libraries

Installing Python Libraries

Best Practices for Using Python Libraries

Section 1.2: Why Python Libraries Matter

1. Rapid Development

2. Community Collaboration

3. Specialized Functionality

4. Cross-Platform Compatibility

5. Extensibility

6. Data Science and Machine Learning

7. Web Development and Automation

8. Large Community and Support

9. Open Source and Free

Section 1.3: Common Python Libraries Overview

NumPy

pandas

Matplotlib

scikit-learn

NLTK (Natural Language Toolkit)

requests

Section 1.4: Installing Python Libraries

Using pip to Install Libraries

Installing Specific Versions

Installing from a Requirements File

Upgrading Libraries

Uninstalling Libraries

Virtual Environments

Summary

Section 1.5: Best Practices for Using Python Libraries

1. Read Documentation

2. Version Compatibility

3. Virtual Environments

4. Keep Libraries Up-to-Date

5. Test Thoroughly

6. Error Handling

7. Dependency Management

8. Contribute to Open Source

9. Understand Licensing

10. Maintain Code Quality

Chapter 2: Getting Started with Standard Libraries

Section 2.1: Overview of Python Standard Libraries

2.1.1. Built-in Functions

2.1.2. Data Types

2.1.3. File I/O

2.1.4. Mathematical Functions

2.1.5. Date and Time

Section 2.2: Working with Built-in Modules

2.2.1. math Module

2.2.2. random Module

2.2.3. datetime Module

2.2.4. os Module

2.2.5. json Module

Section 2.3: Using Data Structures from the Standard Library

2.3.1. Lists

2.3.2. Tuples

2.3.3. Sets

2.3.4. Dictionaries

2.3.5. Collections Module

Section 2.4: Handling Files and I/O Operations

2.4.1. Opening and Closing Files

2.4.2. Reading from Files

2.4.3. Writing to Files

2.4.4. Working with Binary Files

2.4.5. File Iteration

2.4.6. Handling Exceptions

Section 2.5: Exploring Standard Library Documentation

2.5.1. Accessing Documentation

2.5.2. Using the help() Function

2.5.3. Browsing Online Documentation

2.5.4. Understanding Docstrings

2.5.5. Exploring Modules and Functions

2.5.6. Reading Examples

2.5.7. Contributing to Documentation

2.5.8. Online Resources and Tutorials

Chapter 3: NumPy: Numeric Computing with Python

Section 3.1: Introduction to NumPy

3.1.1. Why NumPy?

3.1.2. Installing NumPy

3.1.3. NumPy Arrays

3.1.4. Basic Array Operations

Section 3.2: Working with NumPy Arrays

3.2.1. Array Indexing and Slicing

3.2.2. Array Operations

3.2.3. Array Shape and Dimensions

3.2.4. Universal Functions (ufuncs)

Section 3.3: Array Operations and Functions

3.3.1. Broadcasting

3.3.2. Mathematical and Statistical Functions

3.3.3. Sorting and Filtering

3.3.4. Linear Algebra with NumPy

3.3.5. Random Number Generation

Section 3.4: Broadcasting and Indexing

3.4.1. Broadcasting

3.4.2. Array Indexing

3.4.3. Multi-dimensional Indexing

3.4.4. Indexing with Boolean Arrays

Section 3.5: Advanced NumPy Techniques

3.5.1. Vectorization

3.5.2. Universal Functions (ufuncs)

3.5.3. Broadcasting Revisited

3.5.4. NumPy's Linear Algebra Capabilities

3.5.5. Random Number Generation

Chapter 4: pandas: Data Manipulation and Analysis

Section 4.1: Introduction to pandas

4.1.1. Why pandas?

4.1.2. Getting Started with pandas

4.1.3. Key Concepts in pandas

Section 4.2: Data Structures in pandas

4.2.1. DataFrame

4.2.2. Series

4.2.3. Index

Section 4.3: Data Cleaning and Transformation

4.3.1. Handling Missing Data

4.3.2. Removing Duplicates

4.3.3. Data Transformation

Section 4.4: Data Analysis with pandas

4.4.1. Descriptive Statistics

4.4.2. Grouping and Aggregation

4.4.3. Pivot Tables

4.4.4. Data Visualization with pandas

4.5.2. Resampling and Frequency Conversion

4.5.3. Time-based Indexing

4.5.4. Rolling Windows and Moving Averages

4.5.5. Time Series Visualization

5.1.2. Introduction to Seaborn

5.1.3. Choosing the Right Visualization

Section 5.2: Matplotlib Fundamentals

5.2.1. Creating Basic Plots

5.2.2. Customizing Visuals

5.2.3. Organizing Multiple Subplots

Section 5.3: Creating Custom Visualizations

5.3.1. Customizing Plot Styles

5.3.2. Customizing Colors and Colormaps

5.3.3. Adding Annotations and Text

Section 5.4: Seaborn for Statistical Data Visualization

5.4.1. Seaborn's Data Structures

5.4.2. Statistical Plot Types

5.4.3. Customizing Seaborn Plots

5.4.4. Pair Plots and Heatmaps

Section 5.5: Interactive Visualization with Plotly

5.5.1. Introduction to Plotly

5.5.2. Creating Interactive Scatter Plots

5.5.3. Building Interactive Dashboards with Plotly Dash

5.5.4. Other Interactive Visualizations

ASSISTANT

Section 5.5: Interactive Visualization with Plotly

5.5.1. Installing Plotly

5.5.2. Basic Interactive Plots

5.5.3. Customizing Interactive Plots

5.5.4. Creating Interactive Dashboards

Chapter 6: Working with Dates and Times

Section 6.1: Handling Dates and Times in Python

Basic Concepts

Formatting Dates and Times

Parsing Dates and Times

Date Arithmetic

Conclusion

Section 6.2: The datetime Module

Importing the datetime Module

Creating datetime Objects

Accessing Date and Time Components

Formatting Dates and Times

Parsing Dates and Times

Date Arithmetic and Comparisons

Conclusion

Section 6.3: Time Zones and Localization

Understanding Time Zones

Using pytz to Work with Time Zones

Converting Between Time Zones

Working with UTC

Handling Daylight Saving Time (DST)

Conclusion

Section 6.4: Time Arithmetic and Calculations

Adding and Subtracting Time Intervals

Finding Time Differences

Performing Date-Based Calculations

Rounding and Truncating Datetimes

Conclusion

Section 6.5: Working with Timedeltas

Creating Timedeltas

Performing Arithmetic with Timedeltas

Timedeltas for Date Differences

Converting Timedeltas to Seconds

Timedelta Arithmetic and Comparisons

Conclusion

Chapter 7: Interacting with Databases

Section 7.1: Introduction to Database Interaction

What Is Database Interaction?

Why Database Interaction Matters

Conclusion

Section 7.2: Using SQLite with Python

Why Use SQLite?

Using SQLite with Python

Interacting with Data

Conclusion

Section 7.3: Connecting to Relational Databases

Why Use Relational Databases?

Popular Relational Databases

Using Python Libraries for Database Connection

Example: Connecting to a PostgreSQL Database

Conclusion

Section 7.4: NoSQL Databases and Python

What Are NoSQL Databases?

Types of NoSQL Databases

Python Libraries for NoSQL Databases

Example: Using PyMongo with MongoDB

Conclusion

Section 7.5: Best Practices for Database Access

1. Use Prepared Statements

2. Close Database Connections

3. Use Connection Pools

4. Handle Exceptions Gracefully

5. Implement Data Validation

6. Monitor and Optimize Queries

7. Secure Database Credentials

import os DB_HOST = os.environ.get("DB_HOST") DB_PORT = os.environ.get("DB_PORT") DB_

Chapter 8: Web Scraping and API Integration

Section 8.1: Basics of Web Scraping

Why Web Scraping?

Web Scraping Tools in Python

Basic Web Scraping with Requests and Beautiful Soup

Ethical Considerations

Conclusion

Section 8.2: BeautifulSoup for Parsing HTML

Installing BeautifulSoup

Parsing HTML

Navigating the Parse Tree

Searching by CSS Selectors

Handling Dynamic Content

Conclusion

Section 8.3: Scrapy for Web Crawling

Installing Scrapy

Creating a Scrapy Project

Writing a Scrapy Spider

Running a Scrapy Spider

Scrapy Features

Conclusion

Section 8.4: Working with RESTful APIs

What is a RESTful API?

Making GET Requests with requests

Authenticating with APIs

Handling Pagination

Rate Limiting and Throttling

Error Handling

Conclusion

Section 8.5: Handling Authentication and Rate Limiting

Authentication Methods

Rate Limiting

Conclusion

Chapter 9: Data Serialization and Formats

Section 9.1: Introduction to Data Serialization

What is Data Serialization?

Why Use Data Serialization?

Common Data Serialization Formats

Conclusion

Section 9.2: Working with JSON

JSON Basics

Serializing Python Objects to JSON

Deserializing JSON into Python Objects

Working with JSON Files

Conclusion

Section 9.3: XML and HTML Parsing

Parsing XML with ElementTree

Parsing HTML with BeautifulSoup

HTML Parsing with Requests and BeautifulSoup

Conclusion

Section 9.4: YAML and Other Serialization Formats

Working with YAML in Python

Other Serialization Formats

Section 9.5: Protocol Buffers and Avro

Protocol Buffers (protobuf)

Avro

Chapter 10: Machine Learning with scikit-learn

Section 10.1: Introduction to Machine Learning in Python

Key Concepts in Machine Learning

scikit-learn: Your Swiss Army Knife for ML

Section 10.2: scikit-learn Overview

The Estimator API

Commonly Used scikit-learn Modules

Workflow with scikit-learn

Section 10.3: Data Preprocessing with scikit-learn

Data Scaling and Normalization

Handling Missing Data

Encoding Categorical Data

Feature Engineering

Text Data Processing

Section 10.4: Supervised Learning Algorithms

Classification Algorithms

Regression Algorithms

Section 10.5: Unsupervised Learning Techniques

Clustering

Dimensionality Reduction

Chapter 11: Deep Learning with TensorFlow and Keras

Section 11.1: Deep Learning Fundamentals

What is Deep Learning?

Artificial Neural Networks (ANNs)

Training Neural Networks

Deep Learning Architectures

Deep Learning Frameworks

Section 11.2: Introduction to TensorFlow

What is TensorFlow?

Key Features of TensorFlow

TensorFlow 2.x

Section 11.3: Building Neural Networks with Keras

Key Concepts in Keras

Training and Evaluation

Transfer Learning

Section 11.4: Training Deep Learning Models

Dataset Preparation

Model Training

Model Evaluation

Overfitting and Underfitting

Saving and Loading Models

Section 11.5: Transfer Learning and Model Deployment

How Transfer Learning Works

Applications of Transfer Learning

Model Deployment

Chapter 12: Natural Language Processing with NLTK and spaCy

Section 12.1: Introduction to Natural Language Processing

Key Challenges in NLP

NLTK (Natural Language Toolkit)

Section 12.2: NLTK: Natural Language Toolkit

Installation

Basic Text Processing with NLTK

Text Corpora and Resources

Advanced NLP Tasks

Section 12.3: spaCy: Industrial-Strength NLP

Installation

Basic Text Processing with spaCy

Advanced NLP Capabilities

Efficiency and Production Use

Conclusion

Section 12.4: Text Classification and Sentiment Analysis

Basics of Text Classification

Sentiment Analysis

Practical Implementation

Conclusion

Section 12.5: Named Entity Recognition and Text Parsing

Basics of Named Entity Recognition

Practical Implementation

Text Parsing

Conclusion

Chapter 13: Scientific Computing with SciPy

Section 13.1: Overview of Scientific Computing

Why Scientific Computing?

The Role of SciPy

Getting Started with SciPy

Conclusion

Section 13.2: Numerical Methods with SciPy

Root Finding

Numerical Integration

Linear Algebra

Interpolation

Optimization

Conclusion

Section 13.3: Linear Algebra and Optimization

Linear Algebra with SciPy

Optimization with SciPy

Conclusion

Section 13.4: Signal and Image Processing

Signal Processing with SciPy

Image Processing with SciPy

Conclusion

Section 13.5: Symbolic Mathematics with SymPy

Basic Symbolic Expressions

Solving Equations

Calculus

Linear Algebra

Conclusion

Chapter 14: Data Visualization with Bokeh and Plotly

Section 14.1: Interactive Data Visualization

The Importance of Interactive Visualization

Introduction to Bokeh and Plotly

Getting Started with Bokeh

Exploring Plotly

Conclusion

Section 14.2: Bokeh for Interactive Plots

Basic Scatter Plots

Line Charts

Bar Charts

Conclusion

Section 14.3: Advanced Bokeh Features

Customizing Plot Appearance

Annotations and Labels

Hover Tools

Conclusion

Section 14.4: Creating Dashboards with Plotly

Installing Plotly

Basic Dashboard Components

Conclusion

Section 14.5: Geographic and 3D Visualization

Geographic Visualization

3D Visualization

Conclusion

Chapter 15: Geospatial Data Analysis with GeoPandas

Section 15.1: Introduction to Geospatial Data

Key Concepts in Geospatial Data

Installing GeoPandas

Section 15.2: Geopandas Basics

Importing GeoPandas

GeoDataFrames and GeoSeries

Reading Geospatial Data

Exploring Geospatial Data

Geometry Operations

Plotting Geospatial Data

Section 15.3: Geospatial Data Manipulation

Geometry Transformations

Projections and Coordinate Reference Systems (CRS)

Dissolving Geometries

Geometric Operations on GeoSeries

Geocoding and Reverse Geocoding

Working with MultiGeometries

Section 15.4: Visualization and Mapping

Basic Plotting

Customizing Maps

Choropleth Maps

Overlaying Geometries

Interactive Maps

Exporting Maps

Section 15.5: Spatial Analysis and Geocoding

Spatial Analysis

Geocoding

Spatial Analysis and Geocoding Libraries

Chapter 16: Testing and Debugging in Python

Section 16.1: Importance of Testing and Debugging

Why Testing Matters

The Debugging Process

Types of Testing

Testing Frameworks

Section 16.2: Writing Test Cases with unittest

Creating Test Cases

Running Tests

Assertion Methods

Test Discovery

Section 16.3: Debugging Techniques and Tools

1. Printing Debugging Statements

2. Using pdb - The Python Debugger

3. Using Integrated Development Environments (IDEs)

4. Logging

5. Third-Party Debuggers

Section 16.4: Test Automation with pytest

Installing pytest

Writing Test Functions

Running Tests

Test Discovery

Parametrized Tests

Fixtures

Conclusion

Section 16.5: Continuous Integration and Testing

Why Use Continuous Integration?

Setting Up Continuous Integration

CI Workflow

Continuous Deployment (CD)

Conclusion

Chapter 17: Packaging and Distribution

Section 17.1: Packaging Python Projects

Why Package Python Projects?

The Anatomy of a Python Package

Creating a Python Package

Building and Distributing a Package

Conclusion

Section 17.2: Creating Python Packages

Step 1: Organize Your Code

Step 2: Add __init__.py

Step 3: Write setup.py

Step 4: Write Documentation

Step 5: Specify Dependencies

Step 6: Build the Package

Step 7: Install Locally

Step 8: Distribution (Optional)

Conclusion

Section 17.3: Distribution and Publishing

PyPI (Python Package Index)

Conda (Anaconda/Miniconda)

GitHub

Custom Repositories

Docker

Package Managers

Continuous Integration (CI)

Documentation and Support

Section 17.4: Managing Dependencies with Pip

Understanding Dependencies

Specifying Dependencies

Installing Dependencies

Dependency Management Best Practices

Section 17.5: Best Practices for Packaging

1. Use a Standard Structure

2. Include a README

3. Use Version Control

4. Include a License

5. Package Metadata

6. Testing

7. Document Your Code

8. Continuous Integration

9. Release Workflow

10. Publish to PyPI

Chapter 18: Performance Optimization

Section 18.1: Profiling Python Code

Why Profiling?

Using cProfile

Visualizing Profiling Data

Line Profiling

Memory Profiling

Optimizing Based on Profiling Results

Profiling Best Practices

Section 18.2: Optimizing CPU and Memory Usage

CPU Optimization Techniques

Memory Optimization Techniques

Section 18.3: Cython and Just-In-Time Compilation

Installing Cython

Writing Cython Code

Creating a setup.py Script

Building the Extension

Using the Cython Extension

Profiling and Benchmarking

Section 18.4: Parallel and Concurrent Programming

Parallel Programming

Concurrent Programming

Section 18.5: Performance Tuning Strategies

Profiling

Optimizing CPU and Memory Usage

Cython and Just-In-Time Compilation

Parallel and Concurrent Programming

Performance Tuning Tools

Continuous Monitoring and Testing

Chapter 19: Web Development with Django

Section 19.1: Introduction to Django

Key Features of Django

Django's Architecture

Getting Started with Django

Conclusion

Section 19.2: Building Web Applications with Django

Django Project Structure

Creating Django Apps

Defining Models

Creating Views

Templates

URL Patterns

Development Server

Conclusion

Section 19.3: Working with Models, Views, and Templates in Django

Models and the Database

Django Admin Interface

Views and URL Patterns

Templates

URL Patterns for Detail Views

Conclusion

Section 19.4: Authentication and Security in Django

User Authentication

Access Control and Permissions

Security Best Practices

Conclusion

Section 19.5: Deploying Django Applications

1. Choose a Hosting Provider

2. Set Up a Production Environment

3. Configure Web Server and Database

4. Secure Your Application

5. Set Up Deployment Scripts

6. Monitor and Maintain

7. Scaling

Conclusion

Chapter 20: Flask: Creating Web APIs

Section 20.1: Introduction to Flask

Key Features of Flask:

Getting Started with Flask:

Section 20.2: Building RESTful APIs with Flask

Creating a Basic RESTful API

Handling Request Data

HTTP Methods and Status Codes

Section 20.3: Authentication and Authorization

Implementing Authentication

Implementing Authorization

Section 20.4: Testing and Documentation

Writing Tests with Flask-Testing

Documenting Your Flask API

Section 20.5: Deploying Flask APIs

Deployment Options

Best Practices for Deployment

# Chapter 1: Introduction to Python Libraries

## Section 1.1: What Are Python Libraries?

Python libraries are essential tools for developers and data scientists. They are collections of pre-written code that provide various functionalities, making it easier to perform common tasks in Python programming. These libraries save time and effort by allowing users to leverage existing code rather than starting from scratch.

### Benefits of Python Libraries

Python libraries offer several advantages:

1. **Efficiency**: Libraries provide optimized code for specific tasks, making operations faster and more efficient.
2. **Reusability**: Developers can reuse code from libraries in multiple projects, promoting code modularity and reducing redundancy.
3. **Community Contributions**: Python has a large and active community of developers who contribute to libraries, ensuring that they are well-maintained and up-to-date.
4. **Cross-Platform Compatibility**: Many libraries are designed to work seamlessly across different operating systems, enhancing portability.
5. **Wide Range of Applications**: Python libraries cover a wide spectrum of domains, from data analysis and machine learning to web development and scientific computing.

### Common Python Libraries

Several Python libraries are widely used in various fields:

- **NumPy**: A library for numerical and mathematical operations, particularly with arrays and matrices.

- **pandas**: Used for data manipulation and analysis, providing data structures like DataFrames.

- **Matplotlib**: A popular library for creating static, animated, or interactive visualizations.

- **scikit-learn**: A machine learning library that offers tools for classification, regression, clustering, and more.

- **NLTK (Natural Language Toolkit)**: Designed for natural language processing tasks like text analysis and language understanding.

- **requests**: A library for making HTTP requests, essential for web scraping and API interaction.

## Installing Python Libraries

To install Python libraries, you can use the package manager pip. For example, to install NumPy, you can run:

pip install numpy

This command downloads and installs the NumPy library and its dependencies.

## Best Practices for Using Python Libraries

When using Python libraries, it's essential to follow best practices:

- **Check Documentation**: Refer to the library's documentation for usage instructions and examples.

- **Version Compatibility**: Ensure that the library version is compatible with your Python version.

- **Error Handling**: Implement error handling to gracefully handle exceptions that may arise when using the library.

- **Testing**: Thoroughly test your code when integrating libraries to catch any issues early.

- **Security**: Be mindful of security considerations when using third-party libraries, especially in web applications.

In summary, Python libraries are powerful tools that simplify development and enable you to accomplish various tasks efficiently. This book will explore these libraries in detail, helping you become proficient in their use for a wide range of applications.

## Section 1.2: Why Python Libraries Matter

Python libraries play a pivotal role in the world of programming and data science for several compelling reasons.

### 1. Rapid Development

Python libraries expedite the development process. By providing pre-built functions and modules, they eliminate the need to write complex code from scratch. This accelerates project development, making Python an excellent choice for prototyping and production.

### 2. Community Collaboration

Python has a vast and active community that continually contributes to library development. This collaboration results in high-quality, well-tested libraries that are both robust and reliable. You can leverage the collective knowledge and expertise of the Python community by using these libraries.

## 3. Specialized Functionality

Python libraries offer specialized functionality in various domains. For instance, libraries like NumPy and pandas excel in numerical and data analysis tasks, while libraries like scikit-learn are designed for machine learning. This specialization allows developers to choose the right tool for the job, reducing development time and effort.

## 4. Cross-Platform Compatibility

Python libraries are designed to work seamlessly across different platforms and operating systems. This cross-platform compatibility ensures that code developed using these libraries can be easily deployed on various environments without major modifications.

## 5. Extensibility

Python libraries are extensible. Developers can build custom functions or modules that complement existing libraries, tailoring them to specific project requirements. This extensibility allows for highly customized solutions while still benefiting from the core library's features.

## 6. Data Science and Machine Learning

Python has become the go-to language for data science and machine learning due to its rich ecosystem of libraries. Libraries like NumPy, pandas, Matplotlib, and scikit-learn provide the tools needed for data manipulation, visualization, and machine learning model development.

### 7. Web Development and Automation

Python libraries are not limited to data science; they are also widely used in web development and automation. Libraries like Flask and Django simplify web application development, while libraries like BeautifulSoup and requests facilitate web scraping and API integration.

### 8. Large Community and Support

Python's popularity has led to a large community of developers and extensive online support. If you encounter issues or have questions about a library, you can find solutions through forums, documentation, and community-contributed resources.

### 9. Open Source and Free

Most Python libraries are open source and freely available, making them accessible to developers of all backgrounds. This open-source nature encourages collaboration and innovation within the Python ecosystem.

In conclusion, Python libraries are a cornerstone of Python's success as a versatile and powerful programming language. They simplify development, provide specialized functionality, and foster a collaborative and supportive community, making Python an ideal choice for a wide range of applications. This book will explore these libraries in depth, empowering you to harness their full potential.

## Section 1.3: Common Python Libraries Overview

Python boasts a rich ecosystem of libraries, each catering to specific needs and domains. In this section, we will provide an overview of some of the most commonly used Python libraries, giving you a glimpse of their capabilities and use cases.

## NumPy

**NumPy** stands for Numerical Python and is fundamental for numerical and scientific computing in Python. It provides support for large, multi-dimensional arrays and matrices, along with an extensive collection of mathematical functions to operate on these arrays efficiently. NumPy is widely used in data analysis, machine learning, and scientific research.

```
import numpy as np

# Creating a NumPy array

arr = np.array([1, 2, 3, 4, 5])

print(arr)
```

## pandas

**pandas** is a library built on top of NumPy, designed for data manipulation and analysis. It introduces two primary data structures: Series (for one-dimensional data) and DataFrame (for two-dimensional data). pandas simplifies data cleaning, transformation, and exploration.

```
import pandas as pd

# Creating a DataFrame

data = {'Name': ['Alice', 'Bob', 'Charlie'],

'Age': [25, 30, 35]}

df = pd.DataFrame(data)
```

```
print(df)
```

## Matplotlib

**Matplotlib** is a versatile library for creating static, animated, and interactive visualizations in Python. It provides a wide range of plotting functions to visualize data in various formats, including line plots, scatter plots, bar charts, and more.

```
import matplotlib.pyplot as plt

# Creating a simple line plot

x = [1, 2, 3, 4, 5]

y = [10, 14, 8, 21, 5]

plt.plot(x, y)

plt.xlabel('X-axis')

plt.ylabel('Y-axis')

plt.title('Simple Line Plot')

plt.show()
```

## scikit-learn

**scikit-learn** is a machine learning library that offers tools for data preprocessing, model selection, and evaluation. It includes a wide range of supervised and unsupervised learning algorithms for tasks like classification, regression, clustering, and dimensionality reduction.

```
from sklearn.datasets import load_iris

from sklearn.model_selection import train_test_split
```

```
from sklearn.neighbors import KNeighborsClassifier

# Load the Iris dataset

iris = load_iris()

X_train, X_test, y_train, y_test = train_test_split(iris.data, iris.target, test_size=0.2)

# Create and train a k-nearest neighbors classifier

clf = KNeighborsClassifier(n_neighbors=3)

clf.fit(X_train, y_train)
```

## NLTK (Natural Language Toolkit)

**NLTK** is a comprehensive library for natural language processing (NLP) tasks. It provides tools for text analysis, language understanding, and text processing. NLTK is invaluable for tasks like tokenization, stemming, sentiment analysis, and text classification.

```
import nltk

from nltk.tokenize import word_tokenize

nltk.download('punkt')

# Tokenize a sentence

sentence = "NLTK is a powerful library for natural language processing."

tokens = word_tokenize(sentence)

print(tokens)
```

### requests

The **requests** library simplifies making HTTP requests in Python. It is essential for web scraping, interacting with APIs, and retrieving data from websites.

```
import requests

# Make a GET request to a website

response = requests.get('https://www.example.com')

print(response.text)
```

These are just a few of the many Python libraries available. Each library excels in its respective domain, making Python a versatile language for a wide range of applications. In the following chapters, we will delve deeper into these libraries, exploring their functionalities and use cases.

## Section 1.4: Installing Python Libraries

To harness the power of Python libraries, you need to install them on your system. Fortunately, Python provides a package manager called pip (short for "Pip Installs Packages") that makes it easy to install and manage libraries. In this section, we'll explore how to use pip to install Python libraries.

### Using pip to Install Libraries

The basic syntax for installing a Python library using pip is as follows:

```
pip install library_name
```

Here, library_name is the name of the library you want to install. For example, to install the popular NumPy library, you would run:

pip install numpy

## Installing Specific Versions

You can also specify a particular version of a library to install using pip. This can be useful if your project requires a specific library version for compatibility reasons. To install a specific version, you can specify it along with the library name:

pip install library_name==version_number

For instance, to install NumPy version 1.20.3:

pip install numpy==1.20.3

## Installing from a Requirements File

In real-world projects, you often have a list of libraries and their versions that your project depends on. You can store this information in a text file commonly referred to as a "requirements file." To install libraries listed in a requirements file, use the -r flag with pip:

pip install -r requirements.txt

## Upgrading Libraries

To upgrade a library to the latest version, you can use the —upgrade (or -U) flag with pip:

pip install—upgrade library_name

For example, to upgrade the requests library to the latest version:

pip install—upgrade requests

## Uninstalling Libraries

If you no longer need a library, you can uninstall it using pip:

```
pip uninstall library_name
```

This removes the library and its associated files from your system.

## Virtual Environments

It's a best practice to use virtual environments when working on Python projects. Virtual environments allow you to isolate project dependencies, ensuring that libraries installed for one project do not interfere with others. To create and activate a virtual environment, you can use the venv module or tools like virtualenv.

```
# Create a virtual environment

python -m venv myenv

# Activate the virtual environment (Windows)

myenv\Scripts\activate

# Activate the virtual environment (macOS/Linux)

source myenv/bin/activate
```

Once a virtual environment is activated, you can use pip to install and manage libraries within that environment.

## Summary

In this section, we've covered the basics of installing and managing Python libraries using pip. It's a crucial skill for any Python developer, as libraries extend Python's capabilities and empower you to tackle a wide range of tasks efficiently. As you progress through this book, you'll get hands-on experience installing and working with various Python libraries to accomplish specific tasks and goals.

## Section 1.5: Best Practices for Using Python Libraries

While Python libraries can significantly enhance your development process, it's essential to follow best practices to make the most of them and ensure your projects remain maintainable and error-free. In this section, we'll discuss some best practices for using Python libraries effectively.

### 1. Read Documentation

Before using a library, it's crucial to read its documentation thoroughly. Documentation provides insights into the library's features, usage, and best practices. It often includes examples, explanations, and guidelines that can save you time and help you avoid common mistakes.

### 2. Version Compatibility

Ensure that the library version you're using is compatible with your Python version and other libraries in your project. Incompatibilities can lead to unexpected issues. You can check a library's compatibility in its documentation or on the library's official website.

### 3. Virtual Environments

Always use virtual environments for your Python projects. Virtual environments isolate project dependencies, preventing conflicts between libraries used in different projects. This practice helps maintain a clean and organized development environment.

## 4. Keep Libraries Up-to-Date

Regularly update your Python libraries to benefit from bug fixes, performance improvements, and new features. Outdated libraries may have security vulnerabilities or compatibility issues. Use the pip command with the —upgrade flag to update libraries.

pip install—upgrade library_name

## 5. Test Thoroughly

Testing is crucial when using libraries. Write unit tests and integration tests to verify that the library behaves as expected in your project. Automated testing helps catch issues early and ensures your code works correctly even when library updates occur.

## 6. Error Handling

Implement proper error handling when using libraries. Libraries can raise exceptions or errors, and your code should gracefully handle them. Use try and except blocks to catch and manage exceptions, providing informative error messages.

```
try:

# Code that uses a library

except LibraryError as e:

print(f"An error occurred: {e}")
```

## 7. Dependency Management

Keep track of your project's dependencies by maintaining a requirements file (requirements.txt). This file lists all the libraries your project relies on, along with their versions. It simplifies the process of sharing your project with others and reproducing your development environment.

## 8. Contribute to Open Source

If you encounter issues or bugs in a library, consider contributing to open-source projects by reporting problems, suggesting improvements, or even submitting pull requests. Active participation in the open-source community can lead to a better experience for everyone.

## 9. Understand Licensing

Be aware of the licensing terms of the libraries you use. Some libraries may have specific licensing requirements that could affect how you can use them in your projects, especially in commercial or proprietary software.

## 10. Maintain Code Quality

Follow Python's PEP 8 style guide and maintain clean and readable code. Properly formatted code is easier to understand, share, and collaborate on. Code quality tools like linters and formatters can help enforce coding standards.

In conclusion, Python libraries are powerful tools that can boost your productivity and expand your capabilities as a developer. By following these best practices, you can make the most of these libraries while ensuring the reliability and maintainability of your projects. Keep exploring and learning about new libraries to stay up-to-date with the ever-evolving Python ecosystem.

# Chapter 2: Getting Started with Standard Libraries

## Section 2.1: Overview of Python Standard Libraries

Python comes equipped with a comprehensive standard library that covers a wide range of functionalities. These standard libraries provide essential tools and modules to perform various tasks without the need for additional installations. In this section, we will provide an overview of some of the key areas covered by Python's standard library.

### 2.1.1. Built-in Functions

Python's standard library includes a set of built-in functions that are always available for use. These functions serve fundamental purposes such as performing mathematical operations, working with data types, and handling input and output. Some common built-in functions include print(), len(), input(), range(), and str(). These functions are the building blocks of Python programming and are used extensively in everyday coding.

```
# Using built-in functions

print("Hello, World!")

length = len([1, 2, 3, 4, 5])

user_input = input("Enter your name: ")
```

## 2.1.2. Data Types

Python's standard library includes a variety of built-in data types that make it easy to work with different kinds of data. Common data types include integers (int), floating-point numbers (float), strings (str), lists (list), tuples (tuple), dictionaries (dict), sets (set), and more. These data types are essential for storing and manipulating data in your programs.

```
# Using built-in data types

age = 30

pi = 3.14159

name = "John"

my_list = [1, 2, 3, 4, 5]

my_dict = {'name': 'Alice', 'age': 25}
```

## 2.1.3. File I/O

Python provides modules for reading and writing files, making it easy to work with external data sources. The open() function and the fileinput module allow you to open and manipulate files in various modes, such as reading, writing, and appending. File I/O is crucial for tasks like data processing and text file manipulation.

```
# File I/O with the open() function

with open('example.txt', 'w') as file:

file.write("Hello, Python!")

with open('example.txt', 'r') as file:
```

```
content = file.read()

print(content)
```

### 2.1.4. Mathematical Functions

Python's standard library includes the math module, which provides a wide range of mathematical functions and constants. These functions are useful for tasks like trigonometry, exponentiation, logarithms, and more. The random module is also available for generating random numbers.

```
import math

import random

# Using math functions

pi = math.pi

sqrt_2 = math.sqrt(2)

random_num = random.randint(1, 10)
```

### 2.1.5. Date and Time

The datetime module in Python's standard library offers a convenient way to work with dates and times. It allows you to create, manipulate, and format date and time objects. This module is invaluable for tasks involving time-sensitive data, scheduling, and event handling.

```
import datetime

# Working with date and time

current_datetime = datetime.datetime.now()
```

```
formatted_date = current_datetime.strftime('%Y-%m-%d %H:%M:%S')
```

These are just a few examples of what Python's standard library has to offer. Throughout this book, we will explore various modules and functionalities provided by the standard library in more detail, empowering you to leverage these tools for your Python programming needs.

## Section 2.2: Working with Built-in Modules

Python's standard library includes numerous built-in modules that provide specialized functionality for a wide range of tasks. These modules extend the core capabilities of Python and simplify complex operations. In this section, we will explore some of the commonly used built-in modules and demonstrate their functionalities.

### 2.2.1. math Module

The math module is a powerful tool for mathematical operations. It provides functions for mathematical constants (e.g., pi and e), basic arithmetic operations (e.g., square root and exponentiation), trigonometry (e.g., sine and cosine), logarithms, and more. Let's see some examples:

```
import math

# Calculate the square root

sqrt_value = math.sqrt(25)

# Calculate the sine of an angle in radians

sine_value = math.sin(math.radians(30))

# Calculate the logarithm base 10
```

```
log_value = math.log10(100)

# Get the constant pi

pi_value = math.pi
```

### 2.2.2. random Module

The random module allows you to work with random numbers and perform various randomization tasks. It includes functions for generating random integers, selecting random elements from sequences, and shuffling sequences. Here are a few examples:

```
import random

# Generate a random integer between 1 and 10 (inclusive)

random_num = random.randint(1, 10)

# Select a random element from a list

fruits = ["apple", "banana", "cherry", "date"]

random_fruit = random.choice(fruits)

# Shuffle the elements of a list in place

random.shuffle(fruits)
```

### 2.2.3. datetime Module

The datetime module enables you to work with dates and times. It provides classes for working with dates, times, and date-time combinations. You can create date-time objects, perform arithmetic operations with them, format them as strings, and much more. Here are some examples:

```
import datetime
```

```
# Get the current date and time

current_datetime = datetime.datetime.now()

# Create a date object

my_date = datetime.date(2023, 10, 20)

# Format a date-time as a string

formatted_date = current_datetime.strftime("%Y-%m-%d %H:%M:%S")

# Calculate the difference between two dates

date_diff = my_date - datetime.date(2023, 1, 1)
```

## 2.2.4. os Module

The os module provides functions for interacting with the operating system. It allows you to perform tasks like navigating the file system, creating and deleting directories, checking file existence, and running system commands. Here are some examples:

```
import os

# Get the current working directory

current_directory = os.getcwd()

# List files and directories in a directory

files_in_directory = os.listdir(current_directory)

# Check if a file exists

file_exists = os.path.exists("myfile.txt")

# Create a directory
```

```
os.mkdir("my_directory")

# Delete a file

os.remove("my_file.txt")
```

## 2.2.5. json Module

The json module is used for working with JSON (JavaScript Object Notation) data. It provides functions for encoding Python data structures into JSON format and decoding JSON data into Python objects. This is valuable for data interchange between different systems and platforms:

```
import json

# Convert a Python dictionary to JSON

data = {"name": "Alice", "age": 30}

json_data = json.dumps(data)

# Convert JSON data to a Python dictionary

decoded_data = json.loads('{"name": "Bob", "age": 25}')
```

These are just a few examples of the built-in modules available in Python's standard library. These modules extend Python's capabilities and make it a versatile language for a wide range of tasks. As you work on various projects, you'll likely encounter and explore more of these modules to simplify complex operations and enhance your Python programming skills.

# Section 2.3: Using Data Structures from the Standard Library

Python's standard library includes a variety of built-in data structures that are essential for storing and organizing data efficiently. These data structures are designed to simplify common programming tasks and improve code readability. In this section, we will explore some of the key data structures provided by the standard library.

## 2.3.1. Lists

Lists are one of the most versatile and commonly used data structures in Python. They are ordered collections of elements that can store a mix of different data types. Lists are mutable, meaning you can change their contents (add, remove, or modify elements) after creation.

```
# Creating a list

my_list = [1, 2, 3, 'apple', 'banana']

# Accessing elements by index

first_element = my_list[0]

# Modifying elements

my_list[3] = 'cherry'

# Adding elements to the end of the list

my_list.append('date')

# Removing elements by value

my_list.remove('banana')
```

```
# Checking if an element is in the list

is_present = 'apple' in my_list

# Length of the list

length = len(my_list)
```

### 2.3.2. Tuples

Tuples are similar to lists but are immutable, meaning their contents cannot be changed after creation. They are often used to represent collections of related values. Tuples are defined using parentheses ( ).

```
# Creating a tuple

my_tuple = (1, 2, 3, 'apple', 'banana')

# Accessing elements by index

first_element = my_tuple[0]

# Length of the tuple

length = len(my_tuple)
```

### 2.3.3. Sets

Sets are unordered collections of unique elements. They are useful for tasks like removing duplicates from a list or testing membership of an element in a collection.

```
# Creating a set

my_set = {1, 2, 3, 4, 4, 5}

# Adding elements to the set
```

```
my_set.add(6)

# Removing elements from the set

my_set.remove(3)

# Checking if an element is in the set

is_present = 4 in my_set

# Length of the set

length = len(my_set)
```

### 2.3.4. Dictionaries

Dictionaries are collections of key-value pairs. They provide a way to store and retrieve data efficiently by using keys as unique identifiers for values. Dictionaries are defined using curly braces { }.

```
# Creating a dictionary

my_dict = {'name': 'Alice', 'age': 30, 'city': 'New York'}

# Accessing values by key

name = my_dict['name']

# Modifying values

my_dict['age'] = 31

# Adding new key-value pairs

my_dict['job'] = 'Engineer'

# Removing key-value pairs

del my_dict['city']
```

```
# Checking if a key is in the dictionary
is_present = 'name' in my_dict
# Number of key-value pairs in the dictionary
length = len(my_dict)
```

## 2.3.5. Collections Module

Python's standard library also includes the collections module, which provides specialized data structures beyond the basic built-in types. Some notable data structures from this module include:

- namedtuple: Creates named tuples with named fields for more readable code.
- deque: Double-ended queues for efficient insertion and deletion at both ends.
- Counter: Counts occurrences of elements in an iterable.
- defaultdict: A dictionary with default values for missing keys.

These data structures from the collections module are handy for various programming scenarios.

```
from collections import namedtuple, deque, Counter, defaultdict
# Creating a namedtuple
Person = namedtuple('Person', ['name', 'age'])
alice = Person(name='Alice', age=30)
# Creating a deque
```

```
my_deque = deque([1, 2, 3])

my_deque.append(4)

my_deque.popleft()

# Creating a Counter

my_counter = Counter([1, 2, 3, 2, 1, 3, 4])

# Creating a defaultdict

my_default_dict = defaultdict(int)

my_default_dict['count'] += 1
```

These are some of the fundamental data structures provided by Python's standard library. Choosing the right data structure for your task is essential for efficient and effective programming. As you work on various projects, you'll become more familiar with when and how to use these data structures to solve specific problems.

## Section 2.4: Handling Files and I/O Operations

Working with files and performing input/output (I/O) operations is a common requirement in many programming tasks. Python's standard library provides various modules and functions to handle files, read and write data, and interact with the file system. In this section, we'll explore file handling and I/O operations using Python.

### 2.4.1. Opening and Closing Files

Before performing any operations on a file, you need to open it. Python's built-in open() function is used to open files. It takes two arguments: the file name or path and the mode in which the file should be opened (e.g., read, write, append). Here's how to open and close a file:

```
# Opening a file for reading

file = open('example.txt', 'r')

# Reading the file contents

content = file.read()

# Closing the file

file.close()
```

It's essential to close the file using the close() method when you're done to free up system resources. However, a better practice is to use a with statement, which automatically closes the file when you're done with it:

```
# Using a with statement

with open('example.txt', 'r') as file:

content = file.read()

# File is automatically closed after exiting the block
```

## 2.4.2. Reading from Files

Python provides several methods for reading data from files:

- read(): Reads the entire file as a single string.
- readline(): Reads a single line from the file.
- readlines(): Reads all lines from the file and returns them as a list.

```
with open('example.txt', 'r') as file:
content = file.read() # Reads the entire file
with open('example.txt', 'r') as file:
first_line = file.readline() # Reads the first line
with open('example.txt', 'r') as file:
all_lines = file.readlines() # Reads all lines into a list
```

### 2.4.3. Writing to Files

To write data to a file, open the file in write mode ('w' or 'wb' for binary files) and use methods like write() or writelines():

```
with open('output.txt', 'w') as file:
file.write('Hello, Python!\n')
file.write('This is a new line.')
with open('output.txt', 'a') as file:
file.write('\nThis is appended data.')
```

### 2.4.4. Working with Binary Files

You can work with binary files using modes like 'rb' (read binary) and 'wb' (write binary). Binary files are used for non-text data, such as images, audio, or binary file formats:

```
# Reading a binary file
with open('image.png', 'rb') as binary_file:
binary_data = binary_file.read()
```

```
# Writing to a binary file
with open('output.bin', 'wb') as binary_file:
binary_file.write(b'\x48\x65\x6c\x6c\x6f')
```

## 2.4.5. File Iteration

Python allows you to iterate through the lines of a file using a for loop. This is a memory-efficient way to process large files line by line:

```
with open('example.txt', 'r') as file:
for line in file:
# Process each line
```

## 2.4.6. Handling Exceptions

When working with files, it's essential to handle exceptions that may occur, such as file not found errors or permission issues. Using try and except blocks can help ensure your program doesn't crash due to file-related issues:

```
try:
with open('missing_file.txt', 'r') as file:
content = file.read()
except FileNotFoundError:
print("File not found.")
except Exception as e:
print(f"An error occurred: {e}")
```

These are the fundamentals of handling files and performing I/O operations in Python. Proper file handling is crucial for reading, writing, and manipulating data efficiently in your programs. As you continue to develop Python applications, you'll encounter various scenarios where file handling and I/O operations are essential skills.

## Section 2.5: Exploring Standard Library Documentation

Python's standard library is vast, offering a wide range of modules and functions to accomplish various tasks. To harness the full power of the standard library, it's essential to become proficient at exploring and using its documentation effectively. In this section, we will guide you through the process of exploring Python's standard library documentation.

### 2.5.1. Accessing Documentation

Python's standard library documentation is readily available online at the official Python website (https://docs.python.org/). You can access documentation for different Python versions, so make sure to choose the version that matches the one you're using.

### 2.5.2. Using the help() Function

Python provides a built-in help() function that allows you to access documentation directly from the Python interpreter. You can use it to get information about modules, functions, classes, and methods. Simply pass an object or module as an argument to help():

```
# Accessing help for a module

import math

help(math)
```

```
# Accessing help for a function

help(math.sqrt)
```

Running help() in a Python interactive session will display information about the provided object, including its docstring and available methods.

## 2.5.3. Browsing Online Documentation

The official Python documentation website offers a user-friendly interface to explore the standard library and its modules. You can navigate through the library's modules, view documentation for classes and functions, and search for specific topics. It's a valuable resource when you need detailed information about a specific module or function.

## 2.5.4. Understanding Docstrings

Docstrings are string literals enclosed in triple-quotes that provide information about a module, class, function, or method. They serve as documentation and are accessible via the help() function and tools like Sphinx, which is used to generate documentation from source code.

Here's an example of a function with a docstring:

```
def greet(name):

"""

This function greets the person passed in as a parameter.

Args:

name (str): The name of the person to greet.
```

*Returns:*

*str: A greeting message.*

"""

**return** f"Hello, {name}!"

## 2.5.5. Exploring Modules and Functions

When exploring standard library documentation, you can focus on specific modules or functions that are relevant to your task. For example, if you're working with file I/O, you might want to explore the os and io modules. If you're interested in mathematical operations, the math module is a valuable resource.

You can also use the search functionality on the Python documentation website to find modules or functions by keywords. This is especially helpful when you're not sure which module or function to use.

## 2.5.6. Reading Examples

Python documentation often includes examples that demonstrate how to use modules and functions. Reading these examples can provide valuable insights into how to apply specific functionality in your own code.

For instance, if you're learning how to use the os module to manipulate files and directories, the documentation will typically include code examples that illustrate common use cases like creating directories, listing files, and deleting files.

## 2.5.7. Contributing to Documentation

Python's open-source nature allows developers to contribute to the improvement of documentation. If you find errors or have suggestions for enhancing the documentation for a module or function, you can participate in the Python community by contributing to the documentation. The Python documentation website provides guidance on how to contribute.

## 2.5.8. Online Resources and Tutorials

In addition to the official documentation, you can find various online resources, tutorials, and guides that cover specific modules or libraries within the Python standard library. These resources often provide practical examples and real-world use cases, making it easier to understand and apply the concepts.

Exploring and effectively using Python's standard library documentation is an essential skill for any Python developer. It enables you to leverage the rich set of modules and functions available, saving you time and effort in coding solutions to common problems. As you gain experience, you'll become more proficient at navigating the documentation and incorporating the standard library's capabilities into your projects.

# Chapter 3: NumPy: Numeric Computing with Python

## Section 3.1: Introduction to NumPy

NumPy, short for "Numerical Python," is a fundamental library for numerical and scientific computing in Python. It provides support for large, multi-dimensional arrays and matrices, along with a wide range of high-level mathematical functions to operate on these arrays. NumPy is an essential tool for tasks involving data manipulation, scientific simulations, and machine learning.

### 3.1.1. Why NumPy?

NumPy is popular among data scientists, engineers, and researchers for several reasons:

- **Efficient Array Operations:** NumPy arrays are highly efficient for performing element-wise operations, making it faster than traditional Python lists.

- **Broadcasting:** NumPy allows you to perform operations on arrays of different shapes, intelligently broadcasting values to match the required dimensions.

- **Linear Algebra:** NumPy provides extensive support for linear algebra operations, making it suitable for tasks like matrix multiplication, eigenvalue calculations, and solving linear equations.

- **Interoperability:** NumPy seamlessly integrates with other scientific libraries in Python, such as SciPy (for scientific computing), Matplotlib (for data visualization), and scikit-learn (for machine learning).

### 3.1.2. Installing NumPy

NumPy is not included in Python's standard library, so you need to install it separately. The most common way to install NumPy is using the pip package manager:

```
pip install numpy
```

Once installed, you can import NumPy into your Python programs using the import statement:

```
import numpy as np # 'np' is a common alias for NumPy
```

### 3.1.3. NumPy Arrays

The core data structure in NumPy is the ndarray (short for "n-dimensional array"). NumPy arrays are similar to Python lists but can have multiple dimensions, allowing you to represent matrices and tensors efficiently. You can create NumPy arrays from Python lists or other iterable objects.

```
import numpy as np

# Creating a 1D NumPy array from a list

arr_1d = np.array([1, 2, 3, 4, 5])

# Creating a 2D NumPy array from a list of lists

arr_2d = np.array([[1, 2, 3], [4, 5, 6]])

# Accessing elements in a NumPy array
```

```
element = arr_2d[0, 1] # Accesses the element in the first row, second column
```

NumPy arrays provide many useful attributes and methods for performing operations. You can access the shape of an array using shape, its data type with dtype, and the number of dimensions with ndim.

## 3.1.4. Basic Array Operations

NumPy simplifies many common array operations:

- **Element-Wise Operations:** You can perform element-wise operations like addition, subtraction, multiplication, and division on arrays without writing explicit loops.

```
import numpy as np

arr1 = np.array([1, 2, 3])

arr2 = np.array([4, 5, 6])

result = arr1 + arr2 # Element-wise addition
```

- **Aggregation Functions:** NumPy provides functions like sum(), mean(), max(), and min() for aggregating data in arrays.

```
import numpy as np

data = np.array([1, 2, 3, 4, 5])

total = np.sum(data) # Sum of all elements

average = np.mean(data) # Average of elements
```

```
maximum = np.max(data) # Maximum value

minimum = np.min(data) # Minimum value
```

- **Array Slicing:** NumPy allows you to extract subarrays (slices) of arrays efficiently.

```
import numpy as np

arr = np.array([0, 1, 2, 3, 4, 5])

subarr = arr[2:5] # Extracts elements from index 2 to 4 (inclusive)
```

- **Reshaping Arrays:** You can reshape arrays using the reshape() method.

```
import numpy as np

arr = np.array([1, 2, 3, 4, 5, 6])

reshaped = arr.reshape(2, 3) # Reshapes into a 2x3 array
```

NumPy's ability to handle multi-dimensional arrays and perform operations efficiently makes it an indispensable tool for numerical computing and data analysis. In the following sections of this chapter, we'll delve deeper into NumPy's features and demonstrate how to leverage them for various numerical tasks.

## Section 3.2: Working with NumPy Arrays

In Section 3.1, we introduced NumPy and discussed the basics of creating NumPy arrays. Now, let's explore some common operations and techniques for working with NumPy arrays in more detail.

### 3.2.1. Array Indexing and Slicing

NumPy arrays support powerful indexing and slicing operations, making it easy to access and manipulate specific elements or subsets of an array.

**Indexing:** You can access individual elements of an array by specifying their indices, just like you would with Python lists. NumPy uses zero-based indexing:

```
import numpy as np

arr = np.array([1, 2, 3, 4, 5])

element = arr[2] # Accesses the third element (index 2)
```

**Slicing:** Slicing allows you to extract a portion of an array. You can specify the start and end indices, and NumPy will return the elements within that range.

```
import numpy as np

arr = np.array([1, 2, 3, 4, 5])

subset = arr[1:4] # Extracts elements at indices 1, 2, and 3
```

NumPy also supports advanced slicing, including negative indices and step values. For example, you can use arr[::-1] to reverse an array.

### 3.2.2. Array Operations

NumPy arrays support a wide range of mathematical and logical operations, making it convenient to work with large datasets.

**Element-Wise Operations:** NumPy performs operations element-wise, meaning that operations are applied to corresponding elements of arrays. This behavior simplifies mathematical operations on arrays:

```
import numpy as np

arr1 = np.array([1, 2, 3])

arr2 = np.array([4, 5, 6])

result = arr1 + arr2 # Element-wise addition
```

**Aggregation Functions:** NumPy provides functions for aggregating data within arrays. You can compute sums, means, maxima, minima, and more:

```
import numpy as np

data = np.array([1, 2, 3, 4, 5])

total = np.sum(data) # Sum of all elements

average = np.mean(data) # Average of elements

maximum = np.max(data) # Maximum value

minimum = np.min(data) # Minimum value
```

**Boolean Indexing:** You can use boolean indexing to filter elements in an array based on a condition. This is particularly useful for data filtering and selection:

```
import numpy as np

data = np.array([1, 2, 3, 4, 5])

# Select elements greater than 3

filtered_data = data[data > 3]
```

### 3.2.3. Array Shape and Dimensions

NumPy arrays can have multiple dimensions, allowing you to represent matrices and tensors efficiently. You can inspect and manipulate the shape and dimensions of arrays using attributes and methods:

- **Shape:** The shape attribute returns a tuple representing the dimensions of the array:

```
import numpy as np

arr = np.array([[1, 2, 3], [4, 5, 6]])

shape = arr.shape # Returns (2, 3) for a 2x3 array
```

- **Reshaping:** You can reshape arrays using the reshape() method. This is helpful when you need to change the dimensions of an array:

```
import numpy as np

arr = np.array([1, 2, 3, 4, 5, 6])

reshaped = arr.reshape(2, 3) # Reshapes into a 2x3 array
```

### 3.2.4. Universal Functions (ufuncs)

NumPy includes a wide range of universal functions (ufuncs) that perform element-wise operations efficiently. These functions are optimized for speed and work on arrays of different shapes and sizes. Some common ufuncs include np.sin(), np.cos(), np.exp(), and np.sqrt().

```
import numpy as np
```

```
arr = np.array([1, 2, 3])

result = np.sqrt(arr) # Computes the square root element-wise
```

NumPy's ufuncs provide a concise and efficient way to apply mathematical functions to arrays without writing explicit loops.

In this section, we've explored various aspects of working with NumPy arrays, including indexing, slicing, element-wise operations, aggregation functions, and ufuncs. These capabilities are the building blocks for performing numerical and scientific computations using NumPy. In the following sections of this chapter, we'll delve deeper into specific use cases and advanced features of NumPy.

## Section 3.3: Array Operations and Functions

In this section, we'll explore more advanced array operations and functions available in NumPy. These operations extend the capabilities of NumPy arrays and are essential for performing complex numerical and scientific computations.

### 3.3.1. Broadcasting

NumPy supports broadcasting, a powerful feature that allows you to perform operations on arrays with different shapes. When you perform element-wise operations between arrays of different shapes, NumPy automatically broadcasts the smaller array to match the shape of the larger one.

For example, you can add a scalar to an array or add two arrays with different dimensions:

```
import numpy as np

arr = np.array([1, 2, 3])
```

```
result = arr + 2 # Broadcasting a scalar
```

Broadcasting can also be applied to arrays with different dimensions:

```
import numpy as np

arr1 = np.array([[1, 2, 3], [4, 5, 6]])

arr2 = np.array([10, 20, 30])

result = arr1 + arr2 # Broadcasting a 1D array to a 2D array
```

NumPy follows broadcasting rules to determine how to align and combine the arrays' dimensions, making it a powerful tool for element-wise operations on arrays of different shapes.

## 3.3.2. Mathematical and Statistical Functions

NumPy provides a comprehensive set of mathematical and statistical functions that operate on arrays. These functions are highly optimized and can be applied element-wise.

Some common mathematical functions include:

- np.sin(), np.cos(), np.exp(): Trigonometric and exponential functions.
- np.sqrt(), np.power(), np.log(): Square root, exponentiation, and logarithmic functions.
- np.abs(): Absolute value.
- np.round(), np.floor(), np.ceil(): Rounding and ceiling functions.

```
import numpy as np
```

```
arr = np.array([1, 2, 3, 4, 5])

result = np.square(arr) # Calculates the square of each element
```

For statistical operations, NumPy offers functions like np.mean(), np.sum(), np.min(), np.max(), and np.std() for computing mean, sum, minimum, maximum, and standard deviation, respectively:

```
import numpy as np

data = np.array([10, 20, 30, 40, 50])

mean = np.mean(data) # Computes the mean of the array

std_dev = np.std(data) # Computes the standard deviation
```

### 3.3.3. Sorting and Filtering

NumPy provides functions for sorting arrays and filtering elements based on conditions.

The np.sort() function sorts elements along a specified axis:

```
import numpy as np

arr = np.array([3, 1, 4, 1, 5, 9, 2, 6, 5, 3])

sorted_arr = np.sort(arr) # Sorts the array in ascending order
```

You can also use the argsort() function to get the indices that would sort the array:

```
import numpy as np

arr = np.array([3, 1, 4, 1, 5])

indices = np.argsort(arr) # Returns [1, 3, 0, 2, 4] as the sorted indices
```

Filtering elements based on conditions can be done using boolean indexing:

```
import numpy as np

arr = np.array([1, 2, 3, 4, 5])

filtered_arr = arr[arr > 2] # Filters elements greater than 2
```

### 3.3.4. Linear Algebra with NumPy

NumPy provides extensive support for linear algebra operations, making it a valuable tool for tasks involving matrices and vectors. You can perform matrix multiplication, eigenvalue calculations, and other linear algebra operations efficiently.

Some commonly used linear algebra functions include:

- np.dot(): Matrix multiplication.
- np.linalg.inv(): Matrix inversion.
- np.linalg.eig(): Eigenvalues and eigenvectors.

```
import numpy as np

# Creating matrices

A = np.array([[1, 2], [3, 4]])

B = np.array([[5, 6], [7, 8]])

# Matrix multiplication

result = np.dot(A, B) # Computes the product of A and B
```

NumPy's linear algebra functions are essential for solving systems of linear equations, performing coordinate transformations, and many other applications in science and engineering.

### 3.3.5. Random Number Generation

NumPy includes a random number generation module (np.random) that allows you to generate random numbers and random arrays. You can use it for various tasks, such as generating random samples, shuffling data, or simulating random processes.

Here's an example of generating random numbers:

```
import numpy as np

# Generate random integers between 1 and 10

random_integers = np.random.randint(1, 11, size=5)

# Generate random values from a normal distribution

random_normal = np.random.normal(0, 1, size=5)
```

Random number generation is a valuable feature in statistical simulations, machine learning experiments, and many other areas of scientific computing.

In this section, we've explored advanced array operations and functions provided by NumPy. These capabilities make NumPy a versatile library for performing complex numerical and scientific computations efficiently. As you gain experience with NumPy, you'll discover even more features and techniques that can help you tackle a wide range of numerical and scientific tasks in Python.

## Section 3.4: Broadcasting and Indexing

Broadcasting and indexing are essential techniques for manipulating and accessing elements in NumPy arrays. In this section, we'll delve into these concepts and explore how they can be used effectively in array operations.

### 3.4.1. Broadcasting

Broadcasting is a powerful feature in NumPy that enables element-wise operations on arrays with different shapes, making them compatible for mathematical operations. Broadcasting automatically extends smaller arrays to match the shape of larger arrays, following certain rules:

- If two arrays have a different number of dimensions, the shape of the smaller-dimensional array is padded with ones on the left side.

- If the shape of the two arrays does not match in any dimension, the array with shape equal to 1 in that dimension is stretched to match the other array's shape.

- If neither condition is met, NumPy raises an error.

Here's a simple example of broadcasting:

```
import numpy as np

arr = np.array([1, 2, 3])

result = arr + 2 # Broadcasting a scalar to the array
```

In this case, the scalar 2 is broadcasted to match the shape of arr, resulting in [3, 4, 5].

You can also perform broadcasting with arrays of different dimensions:

```
import numpy as np

arr1 = np.array([[1, 2, 3], [4, 5, 6]])

arr2 = np.array([10, 20, 30])

result = arr1 + arr2 # Broadcasting a 1D array to a 2D array
```

Broadcasting simplifies element-wise operations between arrays of different shapes and is a crucial tool for working with NumPy.

## 3.4.2. Array Indexing

Array indexing in NumPy allows you to access specific elements or subsets of an array. You can use various indexing techniques to retrieve data from arrays.

**Basic Indexing:** You can access individual elements of an array by specifying their indices, similar to Python lists. NumPy uses zero-based indexing:

```
import numpy as np

arr = np.array([1, 2, 3, 4, 5])

element = arr[2] # Accesses the third element (index 2)
```

**Slicing:** Slicing enables you to extract a portion of an array by specifying the start and end indices:

```
import numpy as np

arr = np.array([1, 2, 3, 4, 5])

subset = arr[1:4] # Extracts elements at indices 1, 2, and 3
```

**Boolean Indexing:** You can filter elements based on a condition using boolean indexing:

```
import numpy as np

arr = np.array([1, 2, 3, 4, 5])

# Select elements greater than 2

filtered_arr = arr[arr > 2]
```

**Fancy Indexing:** Fancy indexing allows you to access multiple elements using an array of indices:

```
import numpy as np

arr = np.array([10, 20, 30, 40, 50])

indices = np.array([1, 3, 4])

selected_values = arr[indices] # Returns [20, 40, 50]
```

These indexing techniques provide flexibility and efficiency when working with NumPy arrays. Understanding how to access and manipulate array elements is essential for various data manipulation and analysis tasks.

### 3.4.3. Multi-dimensional Indexing

NumPy supports multi-dimensional indexing, allowing you to access elements in multi-dimensional arrays. You can use commas to separate indices for different dimensions:

```
import numpy as np

arr = np.array([[1, 2, 3], [4, 5, 6], [7, 8, 9]])
```

element = arr[1, 2] # *Accesses the element in the second row and third column*

You can also use slicing with multi-dimensional arrays:

```
import numpy as np

arr = np.array([[1, 2, 3], [4, 5, 6], [7, 8, 9]])

subset = arr[:2, 1:] # Extracts a sub-array from the first two rows and second and third columns
```

Multi-dimensional indexing and slicing are crucial for working with data organized in multi-dimensional arrays, such as images, matrices, and tensors.

### 3.4.4. Indexing with Boolean Arrays

Boolean arrays can be used as masks for indexing to filter elements that satisfy certain conditions. This is particularly useful for data filtering and selection:

```
import numpy as np

data = np.array([1, 2, 3, 4, 5])

# Create a boolean mask for elements greater than 2

mask = data > 2

# Use the mask to select elements from the original array

filtered_data = data[mask] # Returns [3, 4, 5]
```

You can combine multiple conditions using logical operators (& for AND, | for OR) when creating boolean masks for more complex filtering.

Understanding broadcasting and indexing in NumPy is essential for efficiently working with arrays and performing a wide range of data manipulation tasks. These techniques empower you to access, manipulate, and analyze data effectively, making NumPy a versatile library for numerical and scientific computing.

## Section 3.5: Advanced NumPy Techniques

In this section, we'll explore advanced techniques and features provided by NumPy that can significantly enhance your ability to work with arrays and perform complex numerical computations.

### 3.5.1. Vectorization

Vectorization is a fundamental concept in NumPy that allows you to perform operations on entire arrays or large portions of arrays at once, without the need for explicit Python loops. This approach leverages highly optimized C and Fortran code under the hood, making operations much faster than traditional loop-based calculations.

Here's an example of vectorized operations in NumPy:

```
import numpy as np

arr = np.array([1, 2, 3, 4, 5])

result = arr * 2 # Vectorized multiplication by 2
```

In this example, the multiplication is applied element-wise to the entire array, resulting in [2, 4, 6, 8, 10]. Vectorization is not only more concise but also significantly faster for large datasets.

### 3.5.2. Universal Functions (ufuncs)

Universal functions (ufuncs) in NumPy are functions that operate element-wise on arrays. They provide a concise and efficient way to apply mathematical operations to arrays without the need for explicit loops.

NumPy includes a wide range of ufuncs for various mathematical and logical operations, including trigonometric functions, exponentiation, rounding, and more. Some common ufuncs include np.sin(), np.cos(), np.exp(), and np.sqrt().

```
import numpy as np

arr = np.array([1, 2, 3, 4, 5])

result = np.square(arr) # Computes the square of each element
```

Ufuncs can also operate on multi-dimensional arrays, making them versatile for a variety of numerical tasks.

### 3.5.3. Broadcasting Revisited

Broadcasting is a powerful feature in NumPy, as mentioned earlier. It allows for operations on arrays with different shapes, automatically extending smaller arrays to match the shape of larger ones. Broadcasting follows a set of rules, and understanding these rules is crucial for effective use.

The broadcasting rules are as follows:

- If two arrays have a different number of dimensions, the shape of the smaller-dimensional array is padded with ones on the left side.

- If the shape of the two arrays does not match in any dimension, NumPy raises an error.

- When comparing the dimensions of the two arrays element-wise, they must be either equal or one of them must be 1.

Here's an example that showcases these rules:

```
import numpy as np

arr1 = np.array([[1, 2, 3], [4, 5, 6]])

arr2 = np.array([10, 20, 30])

result = arr1 + arr2 # Broadcasting a 1D array to a 2D array
```

Understanding broadcasting allows you to perform element-wise operations efficiently on arrays with different shapes.

### 3.5.4. NumPy's Linear Algebra Capabilities

NumPy provides extensive support for linear algebra operations, making it a valuable tool for tasks involving matrices and vectors. You can perform matrix multiplication, eigenvalue calculations, and other linear algebra operations efficiently.

Some commonly used linear algebra functions include:

- np.dot(): Matrix multiplication.

- np.linalg.inv(): Matrix inversion.

- np.linalg.eig(): Eigenvalues and eigenvectors.

```
import numpy as np
```

```
# Creating matrices

A = np.array([[1, 2], [3, 4]])

B = np.array([[5, 6], [7, 8]])

# Matrix multiplication

result = np.dot(A, B) # Computes the product of A and B
```

These linear algebra functions are essential for solving systems of linear equations, performing coordinate transformations, and many other applications in science and engineering.

## 3.5.5. Random Number Generation

NumPy includes a random number generation module (np.random) that allows you to generate random numbers and random arrays. You can use it for various tasks, such as generating random samples, shuffling data, or simulating random processes.

Here's an example of generating random numbers:

```
import numpy as np

# Generate random integers between 1 and 10

random_integers = np.random.randint(1, 11, size=5)

# Generate random values from a normal distribution

random_normal = np.random.normal(0, 1, size=5)
```

Random number generation is a valuable feature in statistical simulations, machine learning experiments, and many other areas of scientific computing.

These advanced techniques and features in NumPy, including vectorization, ufuncs, broadcasting, linear algebra, and random number generation, make it a versatile library for numerical and scientific computing. Mastering these techniques can significantly enhance your ability to work with arrays and perform complex numerical computations efficiently.

# Chapter 4: pandas: Data Manipulation and Analysis

## Section 4.1: Introduction to pandas

pandas[1] is a widely used Python library for data manipulation and analysis. It provides data structures and functions that make working with structured data, such as spreadsheets or SQL tables, more efficient and intuitive. pandas is built on top of NumPy and is a fundamental tool in the data science ecosystem.

### 4.1.1. Why pandas?

pandas is popular among data scientists and analysts for several reasons:

- **DataFrame:** The central data structure in pandas is the DataFrame, which is a two-dimensional table with labeled axes (rows and columns). This allows for easy representation and manipulation of structured data.

- **Data Cleaning:** pandas provides numerous functions to handle missing data, duplicate entries, and other data cleaning tasks. It makes data preparation for analysis much more manageable.

- **Data Aggregation:** You can perform complex data aggregations and transformations with ease. Grouping data, calculating statistics, and pivoting tables are straightforward operations in pandas.

1. https://pandas.pydata.org/

• **Data Import and Export:** pandas supports reading data from various file formats like CSV, Excel, SQL databases, and more. It also enables easy data export.

• **Integration with Other Libraries:** pandas seamlessly integrates with other Python libraries, such as NumPy, Matplotlib, and scikit-learn, making it a valuable part of the data science ecosystem.

## 4.1.2. Getting Started with pandas

Before using pandas, you'll need to install it if you haven't already. You can install pandas using pip:

```
pip install pandas
```

Once pandas is installed, you can start using it in your Python scripts or Jupyter notebooks.

Here's a basic example of creating a pandas DataFrame:

```
import pandas as pd

# Creating a DataFrame from a dictionary

data = {'Name': ['Alice', 'Bob', 'Charlie', 'David'],

'Age': [25, 30, 35, 40]}

df = pd.DataFrame(data)

print(df)
```

This code creates a simple DataFrame with two columns, 'Name' and 'Age', and four rows of data. You'll notice that pandas automatically assigns row indices (0 to 3) to the DataFrame.

## 4.1.3. Key Concepts in pandas

pandas introduces several key concepts and data structures:

- **DataFrame:** The primary data structure in pandas, representing tabular data. It consists of rows and columns, where each column can have a different data type.

- **Series:** A one-dimensional array-like object in pandas, similar to a single column of a DataFrame. Series objects are used for working with single variables or features.

- **Index:** Each DataFrame and Series has an index, which provides labels for rows or elements. You can use these labels to access specific data points.

- **Data Alignment:** pandas aligns data based on the indices, making it easy to perform operations on data even when the data comes from different sources or has missing values.

- **Data Cleaning:** pandas offers functions for handling missing data (NaN values), filtering, dropping duplicates, and more.

- **Data Selection and Slicing:** You can select and slice data in various ways using row and column labels or by specifying conditions.

In this section, we've introduced pandas, a powerful library for data manipulation and analysis in Python. We discussed why pandas is widely used and its key concepts, including DataFrames, Series, and indices. In the following sections of this chapter, we'll dive deeper into pandas features and techniques for data manipulation and analysis.

## Section 4.2: Data Structures in pandas

In pandas, data is organized into two main data structures: DataFrames and Series. Understanding these data structures is fundamental to working effectively with pandas.

### 4.2.1. DataFrame

A DataFrame is a two-dimensional, size-mutable, and potentially heterogeneous tabular data structure with labeled axes (rows and columns). It can be thought of as a spreadsheet or SQL table. Each column in a DataFrame can have a different data type (e.g., integers, floats, strings, dates).

You can create a DataFrame in various ways, such as from dictionaries, lists, NumPy arrays, or by reading data from external sources like CSV files or databases. Here's an example of creating a DataFrame from a dictionary:

```
import pandas as pd

data = {'Name': ['Alice', 'Bob', 'Charlie', 'David'],

'Age': [25, 30, 35, 40]}

df = pd.DataFrame(data)

print(df)
```

This code snippet creates a simple DataFrame with two columns, 'Name' and 'Age', and displays the following table:

Name Age

0 Alice 25

1 Bob 30

2 Charlie 35

3 David 40

### 4.2.2. Series

A Series is a one-dimensional array-like object that can hold any data type. It is similar to a single column in a DataFrame but with an associated index. You can create a Series from lists, arrays, dictionaries, or other Series objects.

Here's an example of creating a Series from a list:

```
import pandas as pd

ages = [25, 30, 35, 40]

age_series = pd.Series(ages)

print(age_series)
```

This code creates a Series called age_series with the following output:

```
0 25

1 30

2 35

3 40

dtype: int64
```

Notice that the Series has an index (0, 1, 2, 3) associated with each element.

### 4.2.3. Index

Both DataFrames and Series have an index, which is a unique label for each row or element. By default, pandas assigns a numeric index starting from 0, but you can customize the index to be more meaningful, such as using dates, strings, or other labels.

Customizing the index can be useful when you need to reference rows by specific labels or perform operations that involve merging or joining data based on the index.

Here's an example of creating a DataFrame with a custom index:

```
import pandas as pd

data = {'Name': ['Alice', 'Bob', 'Charlie', 'David'],

'Age': [25, 30, 35, 40]}

index_labels = ['A', 'B', 'C', 'D']

df = pd.DataFrame(data, index=index_labels)

print(df)
```

This code creates a DataFrame with a custom index and displays the following table:

```
Name Age

A Alice 25

B Bob 30

C Charlie 35

D David 40
```

Customizing the index makes it easier to reference and work with specific rows or elements in your data.

Understanding DataFrames, Series, and the concept of the index is crucial when working with pandas. These data structures form the foundation for data manipulation and analysis tasks in pandas, and mastering them will enable you to perform various data operations effectively.

## Section 4.3: Data Cleaning and Transformation

Data cleaning and transformation are essential steps in the data analysis process, and pandas provides powerful tools to help you prepare your data for analysis. In this section, we'll explore various data cleaning and transformation techniques using pandas.

### 4.3.1. Handling Missing Data

Dealing with missing data is a common task in data analysis. pandas provides methods to identify and handle missing values effectively. Some key functions for handling missing data include:

- isna() and isnull(): These functions return a DataFrame of the same shape as the input, with Boolean values indicating whether each element is missing (True) or not (False).

- dropna(): This function allows you to remove rows or columns containing missing values.

- fillna(): You can use this function to fill missing values with a specified value or a method like forward-fill or backward-fill.

Here's an example of handling missing data in a DataFrame:

```
import pandas as pd

import numpy as np

data = {'A': [1, 2, np.nan, 4],

'B': [5, np.nan, np.nan, 8],

'C': [9, 10, 11, 12]}

df = pd.DataFrame(data)

# Check for missing values

missing = df.isna()

# Remove rows with missing values

df_cleaned = df.dropna()

# Fill missing values with the mean of each column

df_filled = df.fillna(df.mean())

print("Original DataFrame:")

print(df)

print("\nMissing Values:")

print(missing)

print("\nDataFrame after removing rows with missing values:")

print(df_cleaned)

print("\nDataFrame after filling missing values:")
```

```
print(df_filled)
```

## 4.3.2. Removing Duplicates

Duplicate rows in a dataset can skew your analysis and lead to incorrect results. pandas provides a drop_duplicates() function to remove duplicate rows based on specified columns or all columns.

Here's an example of removing duplicates from a DataFrame:

```
import pandas as pd

data = {'A': [1, 2, 2, 3, 4],

'B': ['X', 'Y', 'Y', 'Z', 'Z']}

df = pd.DataFrame(data)

# Remove duplicate rows based on all columns

df_no_duplicates = df.drop_duplicates()

print("Original DataFrame:")

print(df)

print("\nDataFrame after removing duplicates:")

print(df_no_duplicates)
```

## 4.3.3. Data Transformation

pandas allows you to perform various data transformations, such as filtering, sorting, and reshaping, to prepare your data for analysis. Some common data transformation operations include:

- filter(): This function allows you to select columns based on specified conditions.

- sort_values(): You can use this function to sort the DataFrame by one or more columns.
- pivot(): This function enables you to reshape data from long to wide format or vice versa.

Here's an example of data transformation using pandas:

```
import pandas as pd

data = {'Name': ['Alice', 'Bob', 'Charlie', 'David'],

'Age': [25, 30, 35, 40],

'City': ['New York', 'San Francisco', 'Chicago', 'Los Angeles']}

df = pd.DataFrame(data)

# Filter rows where age is greater than 30

filtered_df = df[df['Age'] > 30]

# Sort the DataFrame by age in descending order

sorted_df = df.sort_values(by='Age', ascending=False)

# Pivot the DataFrame to reshape it

pivot_df = df.pivot(index='Name', columns='City', values='Age')

print("Original DataFrame:")

print(df)

print("\nFiltered DataFrame:")

print(filtered_df)

print("\nSorted DataFrame:")
```

```
print(sorted_df)

print("\nPivoted DataFrame:")

print(pivot_df)
```

These are just a few examples of the data cleaning and transformation capabilities of pandas. Depending on your specific data analysis needs, you can perform a wide range of operations to prepare your data for further analysis and visualization. Understanding these techniques is crucial for effectively working with real-world datasets.

## Section 4.4: Data Analysis with pandas

Once you have cleaned and prepared your data using pandas, the next step is data analysis. pandas provides a wide range of tools and functions for performing data analysis tasks, such as aggregation, grouping, and statistical analysis. In this section, we'll explore some of the key data analysis techniques you can apply using pandas.

### 4.4.1. Descriptive Statistics

pandas offers various methods for calculating descriptive statistics of your data. These statistics provide a summary of the central tendency, dispersion, and shape of your dataset. Some common descriptive statistics functions include:

- mean(): Calculates the mean (average) of numerical columns.

- median(): Computes the median (middle value) of numerical columns.

- std(): Calculates the standard deviation, which measures the spread of data.

- min() and max(): Retrieve the minimum and maximum values in numerical columns.

Here's an example of using these functions to compute descriptive statistics on a DataFrame:

```
import pandas as pd

data = {'Age': [25, 30, 35, 40, 45, 50],

'Income': [50000, 60000, 75000, 80000, 90000, 95000]}

df = pd.DataFrame(data)

# Calculate mean, median, standard deviation, min, and max

mean_age = df['Age'].mean()

median_income = df['Income'].median()

std_age = df['Age'].std()

min_income = df['Income'].min()

max_age = df['Age'].max()

print(f"Mean Age: {mean_age}")

print(f"Median Income: {median_income}")

print(f"Standard Deviation of Age: {std_age}")

print(f"Minimum Income: {min_income}")

print(f"Maximum Age: {max_age}")
```

### 4.4.2. Grouping and Aggregation

pandas allows you to group your data based on one or more columns and perform aggregation operations on the groups. This is particularly useful for summarizing data and gaining insights. You can use the groupby() function to group data and then apply aggregation functions like sum(), mean(), count(), and more.

Here's an example of grouping and aggregation using pandas:

```
import pandas as pd

data = {'Category': ['A', 'B', 'A', 'B', 'A', 'B'],

'Value': [10, 15, 20, 25, 30, 35]}

df = pd.DataFrame(data)

# Group by 'Category' and calculate the mean value for each group

grouped = df.groupby('Category')['Value'].mean()

print(grouped)
```

This code groups the data by the 'Category' column and calculates the mean value for each category, resulting in the following output:

```
Category

A 20.0

B 25.0

Name: Value, dtype: float64
```

### 4.4.3. Pivot Tables

Pivot tables are a powerful way to reshape and summarize data in pandas. You can use the pivot_table() function to create pivot tables that provide insights into your data. Pivot tables allow you to aggregate and cross-tabulate data based on multiple columns.

Here's an example of creating a pivot table in pandas:

```
import pandas as pd

data = {'Category': ['A', 'A', 'B', 'B', 'A', 'B'],

'Month': ['Jan', 'Feb', 'Jan', 'Feb', 'Jan', 'Feb'],

'Value': [10, 15, 20, 25, 30, 35]}

df = pd.DataFrame(data)

# Create a pivot table that summarizes 'Value' by 'Category' and 'Month'

pivot_table = df.pivot_table(index='Category', columns='Month', values='Value', aggfunc='sum')

print(pivot_table)
```

This code creates a pivot table that summarizes the 'Value' column by 'Category' and 'Month', resulting in the following output:

```
Month Feb Jan

Category

A 15 40

B 60 20
```

### 4.4.4. Data Visualization with pandas

pandas also integrates with data visualization libraries like Matplotlib and Seaborn, allowing you to create various charts and plots directly from your DataFrame. This makes it easier to visualize and explore your data.

Here's an example of creating a bar plot using pandas and Matplotlib:

```
import pandas as pd

import matplotlib.pyplot as plt

data = {'Category': ['A', 'B', 'C', 'D'],

'Value': [10, 25, 15, 30]}

df = pd.DataFrame(data)

# Create a bar plot

df.plot(kind='bar', x='Category', y='Value', legend=False)

plt.title('Bar Plot of Categories')

plt.xlabel('Category')

plt.ylabel('Value')

plt.show
```

##

**## Section 4.5: Time Series Analysis with pandas**

**Time series data consists of observations or measurements taken at different points in time, typically at regular intervals. Time**

series analysis is crucial in various fields, including finance, economics, and environmental science. pandas provides powerful tools for working with time series data, making it a valuable library for time series analysis. In this section, we'll explore some of the key techniques for handling and analyzing time series data using pandas.

### 4.5.1. Date and Time Handling

pandas provides the `Timestamp` data type to represent dates and times. You can create a `Timestamp` object from a string or use it as an index for your DataFrame. When working with time series data, it's essential to parse date and time information correctly.

Here's an example of creating a DataFrame with a `DatetimeIndex`:

```python
import pandas as pd

# Create a DataFrame with a DatetimeIndex

date_rng = pd.date_range(start='2023-01-01', end='2023-01-05', freq='D')

df = pd.DataFrame(date_rng, columns=['date'])

print(df)
```

This code creates a DataFrame with a date range from January 1, 2023, to January 5, 2023, with a daily frequency.

### 4.5.2. Resampling and Frequency Conversion

pandas allows you to resample time series data to different frequencies. You can upsample (increase the frequency) or downsample (decrease the frequency) your data based on your analysis needs. This is useful for aggregating data over different time intervals.

Here's an example of resampling time series data:

```
import pandas as pd

# Create a DataFrame with hourly data

date_rng = pd.date_range(start='2023-01-01', end='2023-01-05', freq='H')

df = pd.DataFrame(date_rng, columns=['date'])

df['data'] = range(len(date_rng))

# Resample to daily frequency, summing the values

daily_df = df.resample('D', on='date').sum()

print(daily_df)
```

This code creates a DataFrame with hourly data and then resamples it to a daily frequency, summing the values for each day.

### 4.5.3. Time-based Indexing

When working with time series data, having a time-based index is often helpful for slicing and querying data based on specific time periods. You can set a DatetimeIndex as the index for your DataFrame using the set_index() function.

Here's an example of setting a time-based index:

```
import pandas as pd

# Create a DataFrame with a DatetimeIndex

date_rng = pd.date_range(start='2023-01-01', end='2023-01-05', freq='D')

df = pd.DataFrame(date_rng, columns=['date'])

df['data'] = range(len(date_rng))

# Set the 'date' column as the index

df.set_index('date', inplace=True)

print(df)
```

This code sets the 'date' column as the index, making it easier to perform time-based queries and operations.

### 4.5.4. Rolling Windows and Moving Averages

pandas provides functions for working with rolling windows and calculating moving averages. Rolling windows are used to compute statistics over a sliding window of time periods. This is useful for smoothing data and identifying trends.

Here's an example of calculating a rolling mean:

```
import pandas as pd

# Create a DataFrame with daily data

date_rng = pd.date_range(start='2023-01-01', end='2023-01-10', freq='D')
```

```
df = pd.DataFrame(date_rng, columns=['date'])

df['data'] = [10, 12, 15, 14, 20, 18, 22, 25, 23, 28]

# Calculate a 3-day rolling mean

df['rolling_mean'] = df['data'].rolling(window=3).mean()

print(df)
```

This code calculates a 3-day rolling mean of the 'data' column, smoothing the data.

### 4.5.5. Time Series Visualization

Visualizing time series data is essential for understanding patterns and trends. pandas integrates with data visualization libraries like Matplotlib and Seaborn, allowing you to create various time series plots.

Here's an example of creating a line plot of time series data using pandas and Matplotlib:

```
import pandas as pd

import matplotlib.pyplot as plt

# Create a DataFrame with daily data

date_rng = pd.date_range(start='2023-01-01', end='2023-01-10', freq='D')

df = pd.DataFrame(date_rng, columns=['date'])

df['data'] = [10, 12, 15, 14, 20, 18, 22, 25, 23, 28]

# Plot the time series data
```

plt.figure(figsize=(10, 6))

plt.plot(df['date'], df['data'], marker='o')

plt.title('Time Series Data')

plt

##

# Chapter 5: Matplotlib and Seaborn: Data Visualization

## Section 5.1: Data Visualization Basics

**Data visualization is a fundamental aspect of data analysis and interpretation. It allows you to represent data graphically, making it easier to understand patterns, trends, and insights. In this section, we'll explore the basics of data visualization using the Matplotlib and Seaborn libraries in Python.**

### 5.1.1. Introduction to Matplotlib

**Matplotlib is a widely used Python library for creating static, animated, and interactive visualizations. It provides a high-level interface for drawing attractive and informative plots, charts, and graphs.**

**To get started with Matplotlib, you first need to import it:**

**```python**

**import matplotlib.pyplot as plt**

Once imported, you can create a simple line plot using the plot() function. Here's an example:

*# Data for the plot*

```
x = [1, 2, 3, 4, 5]

y = [10, 12, 5, 8, 3]

# Create a line plot

plt.plot(x, y)

# Add labels to the axes and a title

plt.xlabel('X-axis')

plt.ylabel('Y-axis')

plt.title('Simple Line Plot')

# Show the plot

plt.show()
```

This code creates a basic line plot with labeled axes and a title. Matplotlib provides extensive customization options for adjusting colors, markers, legends, and more to make your plots informative and visually appealing.

## 5.1.2. Introduction to Seaborn

Seaborn is built on top of Matplotlib and provides a high-level interface for creating aesthetically pleasing statistical graphics. It simplifies the process of creating complex visualizations and offers a wide range of built-in themes and color palettes.

To use Seaborn, you need to import it:

```
import seaborn as sns
```

Seaborn is particularly useful for creating statistical plots like histograms, box plots, and violin plots. Here's an example of creating a histogram with Seaborn:

```
# Import Seaborn and set the style

import seaborn as sns

# Sample data

data = [10, 12, 5, 8, 3, 15, 7, 9, 11, 14]

# Create a histogram

sns.histplot(data, bins=5, kde=True)

# Add labels to the axes and a title

plt.xlabel('Value')

plt.ylabel('Frequency')

plt.title('Histogram with Seaborn')

# Show the plot

plt.show()
```

Seaborn's syntax is designed to be intuitive and concise, making it a great choice for exploratory data analysis and statistical visualization.

## 5.1.3. Choosing the Right Visualization

Selecting the appropriate type of visualization for your data is crucial. Different types of plots are suitable for different types of data and analysis goals. Some common types of visualizations include:

- **Line Plots:** Used to display trends over time or show the relationship between two continuous variables.

- **Bar Charts:** Effective for comparing categorical data or showing the distribution of a variable within categories.

- **Histograms:** Used to visualize the distribution of a single variable.

- **Scatter Plots:** Ideal for examining relationships between two continuous variables.

- **Box Plots:** Useful for displaying the distribution of a variable, including measures of central tendency and variability.

- **Heatmaps:** Effective for showing patterns and correlations in large datasets.

Choosing the right visualization can greatly enhance your ability to convey insights from your data. Experimenting with different plot types and styles is a valuable skill for data analysts and scientists.

In this section, we've introduced the basics of data visualization using Matplotlib and Seaborn. These libraries provide a solid foundation for creating a wide range of plots and graphs to explore and communicate your data effectively.

## Section 5.2: Matplotlib Fundamentals

Matplotlib is a powerful library for creating a wide range of static and interactive visualizations in Python. In this section, we'll delve into the fundamentals of Matplotlib, including creating basic plots, customizing visuals, and organizing multiple subplots.

## 5.2.1. Creating Basic Plots

At the core of Matplotlib are the Figure and Axes objects. A Figure is a container for one or more Axes, and each Axes represents an individual plot. To create a basic plot, you typically start by creating a Figure and one or more Axes.

Here's an example of creating a simple line plot using Matplotlib:

```
import matplotlib.pyplot as plt

# Sample data

x = [1, 2, 3, 4, 5]

y = [10, 12, 5, 8, 3]

# Create a Figure and an Axes

fig, ax = plt.subplots()

# Plot the data

ax.plot(x, y)

# Add labels to the axes and a title

ax.set_xlabel('X-axis')

ax.set_ylabel('Y-axis')

ax.set_title('Simple Line Plot')

# Show the plot

plt.show()
```

In this code: - We import Matplotlib as plt. - Sample data x and y are defined. - We create a Figure and an Axes using plt.subplots(). - The data is plotted on the Axes. - Labels and a title are added to the Axes. - Finally, plt.show() displays the plot.

### 5.2.2. Customizing Visuals

Matplotlib offers extensive customization options to modify the appearance of your plots. You can adjust colors, markers, line styles, and more. Here's an example of customizing a line plot:

```
import matplotlib.pyplot as plt

# Sample data

x = [1, 2, 3, 4, 5]

y = [10, 12, 5, 8, 3]

# Create a Figure and an Axes

fig, ax = plt.subplots()

# Plot the data with customizations

ax.plot(x, y, linestyle='—', marker='o', color='blue', label='Data Points')

# Add labels to the axes and a title

ax.set_xlabel('X-axis')

ax.set_ylabel('Y-axis')

ax.set_title('Customized Line Plot')

# Add a legend

ax.legend()

# Show the plot
```

```
plt.show()
```

In this code: - We customize the line style using linestyle, marker style using marker, and line color using color. - A label is added to the plot to be used in the legend. - The legend is displayed using ax.legend().

## 5.2.3. Organizing Multiple Subplots

Matplotlib allows you to create multiple subplots within a single Figure, which is useful for comparing multiple plots or visualizing related data. You can use the subplots() function to create a grid of subplots.

Here's an example of creating multiple subplots:

```
import matplotlib.pyplot as plt

import numpy as np

# Generate sample data

x = np.linspace(0, 10, 100)

y1 = np.sin(x)

y2 = np.cos(x)

# Create a Figure with two subplots

fig, (ax1, ax2) = plt.subplots(1, 2, figsize=(10, 4))

# Plot data on the first subplot

ax1.plot(x, y1, label='sin(x)')

ax1.set_xlabel('X-axis')
```

```
ax1.set_ylabel('Y-axis')

ax1.set_title('Sine Function')

ax1.legend()

# Plot data on the second subplot

ax2.plot(x, y2, label='cos(x)', color='orange')

ax2.set_xlabel('X-axis')

ax2.set_ylabel('Y-axis')

ax2.set_title('Cosine Function')

ax2.legend()

# Adjust spacing between subplots

plt.tight_layout()

# Show the plot

plt.show()
```

In this code: - We create a Figure with two subplots using plt.subplots(1, 2). - Data is plotted on each subplot separately. - Labels, titles, and legends are added to both subplots. - plt.tight_layout() ensures proper spacing between subplots.

These fundamentals of Matplotlib provide a solid foundation for creating a wide range of static visualizations. Matplotlib's flexibility allows you to create custom plots tailored to your specific data and visualization needs.

## Section 5.3: Creating Custom Visualizations

Matplotlib offers a high level of customization to create visually appealing and informative plots tailored to your data and analysis goals. In this section, we'll explore how to customize various aspects of your Matplotlib visualizations.

### 5.3.1. Customizing Plot Styles

Matplotlib provides several built-in styles that you can use to change the overall appearance of your plots. You can set a style using plt.style.use().

Here's an example of applying the "ggplot" style:

```
import matplotlib.pyplot as plt

# Sample data

x = [1, 2, 3, 4, 5]

y = [10, 12, 5, 8, 3]

# Apply the "ggplot" style

plt.style.use('ggplot')

# Create a Figure and an Axes

fig, ax = plt.subplots()

# Plot the data

ax.plot(x, y)

# Add labels to the axes and a title

ax.set_xlabel('X-axis')
```

```
ax.set_ylabel('Y-axis')

ax.set_title('Customized Line Plot with "ggplot" Style')

# Show the plot

plt.show()
```

In this code, the “ggplot” style is applied to the plot, changing the appearance of elements like lines, fonts, and grids. You can explore other built-in styles provided by Matplotlib or create your custom styles.

## 5.3.2. Customizing Colors and Colormaps

You can specify custom colors for lines, markers, and other elements in your plot. Matplotlib supports various color representations, including named colors, RGB tuples, and hexadecimal codes.

Here’s an example of customizing colors:

```
import matplotlib.pyplot as plt

# Sample data

x = [1, 2, 3, 4, 5]

y = [10, 12, 5, 8, 3]

# Create a Figure and an Axes

fig, ax = plt.subplots()

# Plot the data with custom colors

ax.plot(x, y, linestyle='—', marker='o', color='purple', label='Data Points')
```

```
# Add labels to the axes and a title
ax.set_xlabel('X-axis')
ax.set_ylabel('Y-axis')
ax.set_title('Customized Line Plot with Custom Colors')
# Add a legend
ax.legend()
# Show the plot
plt.show()
```

In this example, we set the line color to "purple" using the color parameter. You can specify colors in various ways to match your design preferences.

Matplotlib also provides colormaps that map numerical values to colors, which can be useful for creating heatmaps or other visualizations. You can choose from a variety of colormaps and customize their appearance.

## 5.3.3. Adding Annotations and Text

Annotations and text can enhance the interpretability of your plots. You can add text, arrows, and annotations using functions like ax.text() and ax.annotate().

Here's an example of adding text to a plot:

```
import matplotlib.pyplot as plt
# Sample data
x = [1, 2, 3, 4, 5]
```

```
y = [10, 12, 5, 8, 3]

# Create a Figure and an Axes

fig, ax = plt.subplots()

# Plot the data

ax.plot(x, y)

# Add a text annotation

ax.text(3, 10, 'Important Point', fontsize=12, color='red')

# Add labels to the axes and a title

ax.set_xlabel('X-axis')

ax.set_ylabel('Y-axis')

ax.set_title('Line Plot with Text Annotation')

# Show the plot

plt.show()
```

In this code, we use ax.text() to add a text annotation at coordinates (3, 10) with the text "Important Point" in red.

These are just a few examples of how you can customize Matplotlib visualizations. You can explore further customization options, such as adjusting line styles, marker sizes, axis limits, and tick labels, to create plots that effectively communicate your data and insights.

# Section 5.4: Seaborn for Statistical Data Visualization

Seaborn is a powerful Python library built on top of Matplotlib that specializes in creating informative and attractive statistical data visualizations. It simplifies the process of generating complex statistical plots, making it a valuable tool for data analysts and scientists. In this section, we'll explore how to use Seaborn for various types of statistical visualizations.

## 5.4.1. Seaborn's Data Structures

Seaborn is designed to work seamlessly with Pandas DataFrames. You can directly use DataFrame columns as input for Seaborn plots, making it easy to visualize and analyze your data.

Here's an example of creating a simple Seaborn scatter plot using a DataFrame:

```
import seaborn as sns

import pandas as pd

# Create a DataFrame

data = pd.DataFrame({

'x': [1, 2, 3, 4, 5],

'y': [10, 12, 5, 8, 3]

})

# Create a scatter plot using Seaborn

sns.scatterplot(data=data, x='x', y='y')
```

```
# Set labels and a title

plt.xlabel('X-axis')

plt.ylabel('Y-axis')

plt.title('Seaborn Scatter Plot')

# Show the plot

plt.show()
```

In this code, we create a DataFrame data and use Seaborn's sns.scatterplot() to create a scatter plot, specifying the column names for the x and y-axis.

## 5.4.2. Statistical Plot Types

Seaborn provides a wide range of statistical plot types, including:

- **Scatter Plots:** Visualize the relationship between two variables.
- **Line Plots:** Show trends over time or across categories.
- **Bar Plots:** Compare categories using bars.
- **Histograms:** Display the distribution of a single variable.
- **Box Plots:** Summarize the distribution of a variable, including quartiles and outliers.
- **Violin Plots:** Combine a box plot with a kernel density estimate.

- **Pair Plots:** Create a matrix of scatter plots for multiple variables.
- **Heatmaps:** Visualize a matrix of data using color.
- **Regression Plots:** Plot and visualize regression models.

Here's an example of creating a Seaborn box plot:

```
import seaborn as sns

# Create a DataFrame

data = sns.load_dataset('tips')

# Create a box plot using Seaborn

sns.boxplot(data=data, x='day', y='total_bill')

# Set labels and a title

plt.xlabel('Day of the Week')

plt.ylabel('Total Bill Amount')

plt.title('Seaborn Box Plot')

# Show the plot

plt.show()
```

In this code, we use Seaborn's sns.load_dataset() to load a sample dataset and then create a box plot using sns.boxplot().

### 5.4.3. Customizing Seaborn Plots

Seaborn provides various options for customizing the appearance of your plots. You can change colors, styles, and more to match your preferences.

```
import seaborn as sns

# Create a DataFrame

data = sns.load_dataset('tips')

# Create a violin plot with customizations

sns.violinplot(data=data, x='day', y='total_bill', hue='sex', palette='Set2', split=True)

# Set labels and a title

plt.xlabel('Day of the Week')

plt.ylabel('Total Bill Amount')

plt.title('Customized Seaborn Violin Plot')

# Show the plot

plt.show()
```

In this example, we use palette to set the color palette and split to create split violins based on the 'sex' column.

Seaborn also provides functions for customizing axis labels, titles, legends, and more to make your plots more informative and visually appealing.

### 5.4.4. Pair Plots and Heatmaps

Pair plots are a powerful tool for visualizing relationships between multiple variables in a dataset. Seaborn's sns.pairplot() function creates a matrix of scatter plots for each combination of variables.

```
import seaborn as sns

# Create a DataFrame

data = sns.load_dataset('iris')

# Create a pair plot

sns.pairplot(data=data, hue='species')

# Show the plot

plt.show()
```

In this code, we load the Iris dataset and use sns.pairplot() to create a pair plot, with different colors for each species.

Heatmaps are useful for visualizing matrices of data using color intensity. Seaborn's sns.heatmap() function allows you to create informative heatmaps.

```
import seaborn as sns

# Create a DataFrame

data = sns.load_dataset('flights')

# Pivot the data to create a matrix

flights = data.pivot_table(index='month', columns='year', values='passengers')
```

```
# Create a heatmap

sns.heatmap(data=flights, cmap='YlGnBu', annot=True, fmt='d')

# Set labels and a title

plt.xlabel('Year')

plt.ylabel('Month')

plt.title('Flight Passengers Heatmap')

# Show the plot

plt.show()
```

In this example, we pivot the data to create a matrix of flight passengers and use sns.heatmap() to create a heatmap.

Seaborn's versatility and simplicity make it an excellent choice for exploring and presenting complex statistical relationships in your data. Whether you need to create basic plots or advanced statistical visualizations, Seaborn provides a wide range of tools to help you effectively convey your insights.

## Section 5.5: Interactive Visualization with Plotly

Plotly is a versatile Python library for creating interactive and web-based visualizations. It allows you to build interactive charts, plots, and dashboards that can be shared and explored online. In this section, we'll explore how to use Plotly for interactive data visualization.

## 5.5.1. Introduction to Plotly

Plotly is known for its ability to create dynamic and interactive visualizations. It offers several modules, including Plotly Express for quick and straightforward chart creation and Plotly Graph Objects for more fine-grained control over your plots.

To get started with Plotly, you need to install it and import the library:

```
!pip install plotly

import plotly.express as px
```

## 5.5.2. Creating Interactive Scatter Plots

One of the simplest and most common interactive plots you can create with Plotly is an interactive scatter plot. Here's an example:

```
import plotly.express as px

# Sample data

data = px.data.iris()

# Create an interactive scatter plot

fig = px.scatter(data, x='sepal_width', y='sepal_length', color='species', size='petal_length', hover_name='species')

# Set labels and a title

fig.update_layout(xaxis_title='Sepal Width', yaxis_title='Sepal Length', title='Interactive Scatter Plot')

# Show the plot

fig.show()
```

In this code, we use Plotly Express (px) to create an interactive scatter plot. The hover_name parameter allows you to display additional information when hovering over data points.

### 5.5.3. Building Interactive Dashboards with Plotly Dash

Plotly Dash is an extension of Plotly that enables you to create interactive web applications and dashboards using Python. With Plotly Dash, you can combine various visualizations and controls into a single interactive interface.

Here's a simple example of a Plotly Dash application:

```
import dash

import dash_core_components as dcc

import dash_html_components as html

from dash.dependencies import Input, Output

import plotly.express as px

# Sample data

data = px.data.iris()

# Create a Dash app

app = dash.Dash(__name__)

# Define the app layout

app.layout = html.Div([

dcc.Graph(id='scatter-plot'),
```

```
dcc.Dropdown(
id='dropdown-species',
options=[{'label': species, 'value': species} for species in data['species'].unique()],
value='setosa'
)
])
# Define a callback to update the scatter plot
@app.callback(
Output('scatter-plot', 'figure'),
[Input('dropdown-species', 'value')]
)
def update_scatter_plot(selected_species):
filtered_data = data[data['species'] == selected_species]
fig = px.scatter(filtered_data, x='sepal_width', y='sepal_length', color='species', size='petal_length', hover_name='species')
fig.update_layout(xaxis_title='Sepal Width', yaxis_title='Sepal Length', title='Interactive Scatter Plot')
return fig
# Run the app
if __name__ == '__main__':
```

```
app.run_server(debug=True)
```

In this example, we create a simple Dash app that allows users to select a species from a dropdown menu, and the scatter plot updates accordingly.

### 5.5.4. Other Interactive Visualizations

Plotly offers a wide range of interactive visualizations, including line charts, bar charts, heatmaps, 3D plots, and more. You can explore the Plotly documentation and gallery to discover the full range of interactive chart types and customization options.

Interactive visualizations created with Plotly can be embedded in web pages, shared on platforms like GitHub, and used to build data-driven applications. It's a powerful tool for creating engaging and interactive data presentations.

In summary, Plotly is a valuable library for creating interactive data visualizations and dashboards in Python. Whether you need to explore data interactively, share insights online, or build web applications, Plotly provides the tools to create engaging and interactive data-driven experiences.

# ASSISTANT

## Section 5.5: Interactive Visualization with Plotly

Plotly is a Python library that allows you to create interactive and dynamic visualizations for data exploration and presentation. It provides a wide range of chart types and customization options, making it a powerful tool for creating engaging and interactive data visualizations. In this section, we'll explore how to use Plotly to create interactive plots.

## 5.5.1. Installing Plotly

To get started with Plotly, you need to install the library. You can do this using pip:

```
pip install plotly
```

Once Plotly is installed, you can import it into your Python script or notebook to start creating interactive plots.

## 5.5.2. Basic Interactive Plots

Plotly makes it easy to create interactive versions of common plot types like scatter plots, line charts, bar charts, and more. Here's an example of creating an interactive scatter plot with Plotly:

```
import plotly.express as px

# Sample data

import pandas as pd

data = pd.DataFrame({

'x': [1, 2, 3, 4, 5],

'y': [10, 12, 5, 8, 3]

})

# Create an interactive scatter plot with Plotly Express

fig = px.scatter(data, x='x', y='y', title='Interactive Scatter Plot')

# Show the plot
```

```
fig.show()
```

In this code, we use Plotly Express, a high-level interface for creating interactive plots. The px.scatter() function creates a scatter plot, and fig.show() displays the interactive plot.

### 5.5.3. Customizing Interactive Plots

Plotly provides extensive customization options to tailor your interactive plots to your needs. You can customize colors, markers, labels, titles, and more.

```
import plotly.express as px

# Sample data

data = pd.DataFrame({

'x': [1, 2, 3, 4, 5],

'y': [10, 12, 5, 8, 3]

})

# Create a customized interactive scatter plot

fig = px.scatter(data, x='x', y='y', title='Customized Scatter Plot',

color_discrete_sequence=['green'], labels={'x': 'X-axis', 'y': 'Y-axis'})

# Show the plot

fig.show()
```

In this example, we customize the scatter plot by specifying the color, labels for the axes, and a title.

## 5.5.4. Creating Interactive Dashboards

Plotly can also be used to create interactive dashboards by combining multiple visualizations and controls. Dash is a Python framework for building web applications, including interactive data dashboards, using Plotly components.

Here's a simple example of a Plotly Dash application:

```
import dash

import dash_core_components as dcc

import dash_html_components as html

from dash.dependencies import Input, Output

import plotly.express as px

# Sample data

data = pd.DataFrame({

'x': [1, 2, 3, 4, 5],

'y': [10, 12, 5, 8, 3]

})

# Create a Dash application

app = dash.Dash(__name__)

# Define the layout of the app

app.layout = html.Div([

html.H1('Interactive Dash App'),
```

```
dcc.Graph(id='scatter-plot'),
dcc.Slider(id='slider', min=1, max=5, step=1, value=3),
])
# Define callback to update the scatter plot
@app.callback(
Output('scatter-plot', 'figure'),
[Input('slider', 'value')]
)
def update_scatter_plot(selected_value):
filtered_data = data[data['x'] <= selected_value]
fig = px.scatter(filtered_data, x='x', y='y', title='Interactive Scatter Plot')
return fig
# Run the app
if __name__ == '__main__':
app.run_server(debug=True)
```

In this example, we create a simple Dash app with a scatter plot and a slider control. The slider control allows you to filter the data displayed in the scatter plot interactively.

Plotly and Dash together provide a powerful framework for building interactive data applications and dashboards, allowing you to create engaging and dynamic data visualizations for your audience.

# Chapter 6: Working with Dates and Times

## Section 6.1: Handling Dates and Times in Python

Working with dates and times is a common task in programming, and Python provides several libraries and modules to facilitate this. In this section, we'll explore how to handle dates and times in Python, including basic operations, formatting, and conversion between different representations.

### Basic Concepts

In Python, the core module for working with dates and times is datetime, which is part of the standard library. You can start by importing it:

```
from datetime import datetime
```

*Creating Datetime Objects*

You can create datetime objects to represent specific dates and times. Here's how to create a datetime object for the current date and time:

```
current_datetime = datetime.now()

print(current_datetime)
```

*Accessing Date and Time Components*

Once you have a datetime object, you can access its components, such as the year, month, day, hour, minute, and second:

year = current_datetime.year

month = current_datetime.month

day = current_datetime.day

hour = current_datetime.hour

minute = current_datetime.minute

second = current_datetime.second

print(f"Year: {year}, Month: {month}, Day: {day}")

print(f"Hour: {hour}, Minute: {minute}, Second: {second}")

## Formatting Dates and Times

You can format datetime objects into human-readable strings using the strftime method. This method allows you to specify a format string with placeholders for various components.

formatted_date = current_datetime.strftime("%Y-%m-%d")

formatted_time = current_datetime.strftime("%H:%M:%S")

print(f"Formatted Date: {formatted_date}")

print(f"Formatted Time: {formatted_time}")

The placeholders in the format string include: - %Y for the year with century as a decimal number. - %m for the month as a zero-padded decimal number. - %d for the day of the month as a zero-padded decimal number. - %H for the hour (24-hour clock) as a zero-padded decimal number. - %M for the minute as a zero-padded decimal number. - %S for the second as a zero-padded decimal number.

## Parsing Dates and Times

To convert a formatted date or time string back into a datetime object, you can use the strptime function. This function parses a string according to a specified format.

```
date_string = "2023-10-15"

parsed_date = datetime.strptime(date_string, "%Y-%m-%d")

print(f"Parsed Date: {parsed_date}")
```

## Date Arithmetic

Python allows you to perform arithmetic operations with datetime objects. For example, you can calculate the difference between two dates:

```
from datetime import timedelta

date1 = datetime(2023, 10, 15)

date2 = datetime(2023, 10, 10)

difference = date1 - date2

print(f"Date Difference: {difference}")
```

This code snippet calculates the difference between date1 and date2 as a timedelta object.

## Conclusion

Handling dates and times is an essential skill in programming, and Python's datetime module makes it relatively straightforward. Whether you need to represent specific moments, format dates for display, or perform date arithmetic, Python provides the necessary tools to work with dates and times effectively.

## Section 6.2: The datetime Module

Python's datetime module is a powerful library for working with dates and times. In this section, we will explore the datetime module in detail, covering various features and functionalities.

### Importing the datetime Module

To get started with the datetime module, you need to import it into your Python script or interactive session:

```
from datetime import datetime
```

This import statement allows you to use the datetime class and related functions in your code.

### Creating datetime Objects

The primary purpose of the datetime module is to work with date and time information. You can create datetime objects to represent specific moments in time. For example, to create a datetime object for the current date and time, you can use the datetime.now() function:

```
current_datetime = datetime.now()

print(current_datetime)
```

This code snippet creates a datetime object representing the current date and time when the code is executed.

## Accessing Date and Time Components

You can access individual components of a datetime object, such as the year, month, day, hour, minute, and second. Here's how you can do it:

```
year = current_datetime.year

month = current_datetime.month

day = current_datetime.day

hour = current_datetime.hour

minute = current_datetime.minute

second = current_datetime.second

print(f"Year: {year}, Month: {month}, Day: {day}")

print(f"Hour: {hour}, Minute: {minute}, Second: {second}")
```

By accessing these components, you can extract specific information from a datetime object for further processing or display.

## Formatting Dates and Times

The datetime module allows you to format datetime objects into human-readable strings using the strftime method. This method takes a format string with placeholders for various date and time components and returns a formatted string.

Here's an example of formatting a datetime object as a string:

```
formatted_date = current_datetime.strftime("%Y-%m-%d")

formatted_time = current_datetime.strftime("%H:%M:%S")
```

```
print(f"Formatted Date: {formatted_date}")

print(f"Formatted Time: {formatted_time}")
```

In this example, the %Y, %m, %d, %H, %M, and %S placeholders represent the year, month, day, hour, minute, and second, respectively.

## Parsing Dates and Times

Conversely, you can parse formatted date and time strings into datetime objects using the strptime function. This function takes a string and a format specifier and returns a datetime object.

Here's how you can parse a date string into a datetime object:

```
date_string = "2023-10-15"

parsed_date = datetime.strptime(date_string, "%Y-%m-%d")

print(f"Parsed Date: {parsed_date}")
```

The strptime function allows you to convert date and time strings from various formats into datetime objects for manipulation.

## Date Arithmetic and Comparisons

Python's datetime module also supports arithmetic operations and comparisons between datetime objects. You can calculate time intervals, perform additions and subtractions, and compare dates and times.

For example, you can calculate the difference between two dates:

```
from datetime import timedelta

date1 = datetime(2023, 10, 15)
```

```
date2 = datetime(2023, 10, 10)

difference = date1 - date2

print(f"Date Difference: {difference}")
```

The result is a timedelta object representing the time interval between date1 and date2.

### Conclusion

The datetime module is a versatile library for handling dates and times in Python. It provides essential functionalities for creating, formatting, parsing, and performing operations on datetime objects. Whether you're working with time-sensitive data, calculating durations, or formatting dates for display, the datetime module is a valuable tool in your Python programming arsenal.

## Section 6.3: Time Zones and Localization

Working with time zones and localization is crucial when dealing with date and time information in a global context. Python's datetime module provides features for handling time zones and localizing datetime objects. In this section, we will explore how to work with time zones and ensure proper localization of datetime data.

### Understanding Time Zones

A time zone is a region of the Earth where the same standard time is used. Each time zone is usually represented by a unique name and an offset from Coordinated Universal Time (UTC) or Greenwich Mean Time (GMT). Time zones account for the Earth's rotation and the variation in time across different longitudes.

Python's pytz library is a popular choice for working with time zones. You can install it using pip:

```
pip install pytz
```

## Using pytz to Work with Time Zones

To work with time zones using pytz, you first need to import the library and create a timezone object. Here's how to create a timezone object for the Eastern Time Zone (US/Eastern):

```
import pytz

eastern_timezone = pytz.timezone("US/Eastern")
```

You can then localize a datetime object to a specific time zone using the astimezone method:

```
from datetime import datetime

current_datetime = datetime.now()

localized_datetime = eastern_timezone.localize(current_datetime)

print(localized_datetime)
```

The localized_datetime object now contains the current date and time information, but it is associated with the Eastern Time Zone.

## Converting Between Time Zones

You can also convert datetime objects between different time zones using pytz. For example, if you have a localized datetime in the Eastern Time Zone and want to convert it to the Pacific Time Zone:

```
pacific_timezone = pytz.timezone("US/Pacific")
```

```
pacific_datetime =
localized_datetime.astimezone(pacific_timezone)

print(pacific_datetime)
```

This code snippet converts the localized_datetime object from the Eastern Time Zone to the Pacific Time Zone.

## Working with UTC

UTC is a commonly used time standard in programming and serves as a reference for other time zones. Python's pytz library provides a UTC timezone object that you can use for operations involving UTC time:

```
import pytz

utc_timezone = pytz.UTC

current_datetime = datetime.now()

# Localize to UTC

utc_datetime = utc_timezone.localize(current_datetime)

print(utc_datetime)
```

## Handling Daylight Saving Time (DST)

Some time zones observe Daylight Saving Time (DST), where the local time is adjusted forward or backward by one hour during certain periods of the year. pytz handles DST transitions automatically, ensuring accurate conversions and calculations.

## Conclusion

Working with time zones and localization is essential for accurate and reliable datetime handling in Python. The pytz library simplifies the process of managing time zones, allowing you to create, localize, and convert datetime objects with ease. Whether you need to display times in different regions, perform calculations across time zones, or work with UTC as a reference, Python's datetime and pytz libraries provide the tools to handle time-related tasks effectively.

# Section 6.4: Time Arithmetic and Calculations

Performing time arithmetic and calculations is a common requirement when working with datetime objects in Python. This section will delve into various aspects of time arithmetic and calculations, such as adding or subtracting time intervals, finding time differences, and performing date-based calculations.

## Adding and Subtracting Time Intervals

Python's datetime module allows you to perform arithmetic operations with datetime objects using timedelta objects. Timedelta objects represent a duration or time interval. You can add or subtract timedelta objects to/from datetime objects to calculate new dates and times.

Here's an example of adding a timedelta of 3 days to the current datetime:

```
from datetime import datetime, timedelta

current_datetime = datetime.now()

three_days = timedelta(days=3)
```

```
new_datetime = current_datetime + three_days

print(new_datetime)
```

This code snippet adds three days to the current datetime, resulting in a new datetime object.

## Finding Time Differences

You can also calculate the difference between two datetime objects to determine the time duration between them. This is often useful for measuring time intervals.

```
from datetime import datetime, timedelta

start_datetime = datetime(2023, 10, 15, 10, 0)

end_datetime = datetime(2023, 10, 18, 15, 30)

time_difference = end_datetime - start_datetime

print(time_difference)
```

The time_difference variable contains a timedelta object representing the duration between start_datetime and end_datetime.

## Performing Date-Based Calculations

Python's datetime module also provides functions for performing date-based calculations. For example, you can calculate the date that is a certain number of days from a given date:

```
from datetime import datetime, timedelta

start_date = datetime(2023, 10, 15)

days_to_add = timedelta(days=7)
```

```
new_date = start_date + days_to_add

print(new_date)
```

In this example, we add 7 days to the start_date, resulting in a new date.

## Rounding and Truncating Datetimes

You can round or truncate datetime objects to a specific unit of time, such as days, hours, or minutes, using various methods. For instance, to round a datetime to the nearest hour:

```
from datetime import datetime

current_datetime = datetime.now()

rounded_datetime = current_datetime.replace(minute=0, second=0, microsecond=0)

print(rounded_datetime)
```

The replace method is used here to set the minute, second, and microsecond components to zero, effectively rounding the datetime to the nearest hour.

## Conclusion

Time arithmetic and calculations are essential when working with datetime objects in Python. Whether you need to add or subtract time intervals, find time differences, perform date-based calculations, or round/truncate datetimes to specific units, Python's datetime module and timedelta objects provide the necessary tools for handling various time-related tasks. These capabilities are valuable for a wide range of applications, from scheduling and event management to data analysis and reporting.

## Section 6.5: Working with Timedeltas

Timedeltas are a fundamental concept in Python's datetime module. They represent the duration between two datetime points and are useful for various time-related calculations and manipulations. In this section, we'll explore how to work with timedeltas in Python.

### Creating Timedeltas

You can create timedeltas directly using the timedelta class from the datetime module. A timedelta can represent a duration in terms of days, seconds, microseconds, milliseconds, minutes, hours, or weeks.

Here's an example of creating a timedelta representing 2 days and 3 hours:

```
from datetime import timedelta

delta = timedelta(days=2, hours=3)

print(delta)
```

The delta object now represents a duration of 2 days and 3 hours.

### Performing Arithmetic with Timedeltas

Timedeltas can be added or subtracted from datetime objects to perform arithmetic operations. For instance, you can calculate the datetime that is 5 hours and 30 minutes from now:

```
from datetime import datetime, timedelta

current_datetime = datetime.now()

delta = timedelta(hours=5, minutes=30)

new_datetime = current_datetime + delta
```

```
print(new_datetime)
```

In this example, the delta is added to the current_datetime to obtain the new datetime.

## Timedeltas for Date Differences

Timedeltas are commonly used to calculate the difference between two datetime objects. This is useful for measuring durations or intervals between events.

```
from datetime import datetime, timedelta

start_datetime = datetime(2023, 10, 15)

end_datetime = datetime(2023, 10, 20)

time_difference = end_datetime - start_datetime

print(time_difference)
```

The time_difference object now represents the duration between start_datetime and end_datetime.

## Converting Timedeltas to Seconds

You can convert a timedelta into seconds, which is a frequently used unit of time in programming. To do this, you can access the total_seconds() method of the timedelta:

```
from datetime import timedelta

delta = timedelta(hours=2, minutes=30)

seconds = delta.total_seconds()

print(seconds)
```

The seconds variable now holds the total number of seconds in the delta timedelta.

## Timedelta Arithmetic and Comparisons

Timedeltas support various arithmetic operations like addition, subtraction, multiplication, and division. You can also compare timedeltas for equality, inequality, and ordering.

```
from datetime import timedelta

delta1 = timedelta(days=2)

delta2 = timedelta(hours=48)

result1 = delta1 == delta2 # True, because they represent the same duration

result2 = delta1 < delta2 # False, because delta1 is shorter than delta2
```

These operations allow you to perform precise calculations involving time intervals.

## Conclusion

Timedeltas are a versatile and essential component of Python's datetime module. They enable you to work with durations and time intervals efficiently, making them valuable for tasks involving time-based calculations, scheduling, and date arithmetic. Whether you need to measure time differences, add or subtract time intervals, or convert durations to different units, timedeltas provide the necessary functionality for accurate datetime manipulation in Python.

# Chapter 7: Interacting with Databases

## Section 7.1: Introduction to Database Interaction

Databases are integral to many applications, allowing you to store, retrieve, and manage structured data efficiently. In this section, we will introduce the concept of database interaction using Python and explore why it's essential for various software projects.

### What Is Database Interaction?

Database interaction, also known as database connectivity, refers to the process of connecting and communicating with a database system using a programming language, in this case, Python. It involves performing operations such as inserting, updating, retrieving, and deleting data from a database.

Python provides several libraries and modules that simplify database interaction, making it easier for developers to work with databases without delving into the intricacies of database management systems (DBMS). These libraries include but are not limited to:

- **SQLite**: A lightweight, serverless, and self-contained database engine often used for embedded and local storage.
- **SQLAlchemy**: A powerful and versatile SQL toolkit and Object-Relational Mapping (ORM) library that works with multiple database systems.

- **Django ORM**: A high-level ORM provided by the Django web framework for building web applications with database support.

- **Third-party database drivers**: Python has many third-party drivers that enable connection to popular DBMS like MySQL, PostgreSQL, and MongoDB.

## Why Database Interaction Matters

Database interaction is essential for several reasons:

1. **Data Storage**: Databases provide a structured and organized way to store data persistently. Applications rely on databases to store user information, product catalogs, transaction records, and more.
2. **Data Retrieval**: Applications need to retrieve specific data quickly and efficiently. Database interaction allows developers to query databases to retrieve the required information.
3. **Data Manipulation**: Users interact with applications by creating, updating, and deleting data. Database interaction enables these CRUD (Create, Read, Update, Delete) operations.
4. **Data Security**: Databases often contain sensitive information. Proper database interaction ensures data security by implementing access controls and encryption.
5. **Scalability**: As an application grows, so does its data. Database interaction techniques and tools help manage data scalability and ensure that applications perform well as the dataset expands.
6. **Concurrency**: Multiple users may access an application simultaneously. Database interaction ensures data integrity

and prevents conflicts when multiple users attempt to modify the same data.

7. **Reporting and Analytics**: Many applications require generating reports and performing data analysis. Database interaction allows developers to extract and manipulate data for reporting purposes.

## Conclusion

Database interaction is a crucial aspect of software development, enabling applications to store, manage, and retrieve data effectively. Python offers a variety of tools and libraries to simplify the process of connecting to databases and performing database operations. Whether you're building a web application, a desktop software, or a data analysis tool, understanding how to interact with databases in Python is a valuable skill for any developer. In the following sections, we will delve deeper into various aspects of database interaction, including working with SQLite, connecting to relational databases, and interacting with NoSQL databases.

# Section 7.2: Using SQLite with Python

SQLite is a lightweight, serverless, and self-contained relational database engine that is widely used for embedded and local storage in applications. In this section, we'll explore how to use SQLite with Python for database interaction.

## Why Use SQLite?

SQLite is an excellent choice for certain scenarios, such as:

1. **Embedded Databases**: SQLite is often used in embedded systems and mobile applications because it requires minimal setup and doesn't rely on a separate server process.

The entire database is stored in a single file, making it easy to distribute.

2. **Local Storage**: When you need to store data locally on a user's device, SQLite provides a simple and efficient way to create and manage databases.
3. **Prototyping and Testing**: SQLite is great for prototyping and testing database-driven applications because it's lightweight and doesn't require complex database server setups.

## Using SQLite with Python

Python includes a built-in module called sqlite3 that provides a straightforward way to work with SQLite databases. Here are the basic steps to use SQLite with Python:

1. **Import the sqlite3 Module**: Begin by importing the sqlite3 module, which comes pre-installed with Python.

```
import sqlite3
```

1. **Connect to a Database**: Use the connect() method to establish a connection to an SQLite database file. If the file doesn't exist, SQLite will create it.

```
# Connect to an SQLite database or create one if it doesn't exist

conn = sqlite3.connect("mydatabase.db")
```

1. **Create a Cursor**: A cursor is an object that allows you to interact with the database. You can execute SQL commands through the cursor.

```
# Create a cursor
```

cursor = conn.cursor()

1. **Execute SQL Commands**: You can execute SQL commands using the cursor's execute() method. For example, to create a table:

*# Create a table*

cursor.execute('''CREATE TABLE IF NOT EXISTS users (id INTEGER PRIMARY KEY, name TEXT, email TEXT)''')

1. **Commit Changes and Close the Connection**: After executing SQL commands, it's important to commit the changes to the database using the commit() method. Finally, close the database connection.

*# Commit changes and close the connection*

conn.commit()

conn.close()

## Interacting with Data

Once you have created a table, you can insert, update, retrieve, and delete data using SQL commands through the cursor. Here's a brief overview:

- **Inserting Data:**

*# Insert data into the table*

cursor.execute("INSERT INTO users (name, email) VALUES (?, ?)", ("Alice", "alice@example.com"))

- **Retrieving Data:**

```
# Retrieve data from the table
cursor.execute("SELECT * FROM users")
rows = cursor.fetchall()
for row in rows:
print(row)
```

- **Updating Data:**

```
# Update data in the table
cursor.execute("UPDATE users SET email = ? WHERE name = ?", ("new_email@example.com", "Alice"))
```

- **Deleting Data:**

```
# Delete data from the table
cursor.execute("DELETE FROM users WHERE name = ?", ("Alice",))
```

Remember to commit changes and close the connection after executing these operations.

## Conclusion

SQLite is a versatile and lightweight database engine that can be easily integrated into Python applications. It's a practical choice for local storage, prototyping, and small-scale database needs. By using the sqlite3 module in Python, you can connect to SQLite databases, create tables, and interact with data using SQL commands. In the following sections, we'll explore more advanced topics related to database interaction, including connecting to other relational databases and working with NoSQL databases in Python.

## Section 7.3: Connecting to Relational Databases

In addition to SQLite, Python provides several libraries and modules that allow you to connect to and interact with various relational database management systems (RDBMS). In this section, we'll explore how to connect to relational databases using Python.

### Why Use Relational Databases?

Relational databases are widely used in software development because they offer the following benefits:

1. **Structured Data**: Relational databases organize data into structured tables, making it easy to represent and query data in a structured way.
2. **Data Integrity**: RDBMS systems enforce data integrity through constraints, relationships, and validation rules, ensuring data accuracy.
3. **Scalability**: Many relational databases can handle large datasets and support concurrent access by multiple users.
4. **ACID Properties**: RDBMS systems adhere to ACID (Atomicity, Consistency, Isolation, Durability) properties, ensuring data reliability and transactional integrity.
5. **Standardized Query Language**: SQL (Structured Query Language) provides a standard way to query and manipulate data in relational databases.

## Popular Relational Databases

Python supports connecting to various relational databases, including:

- **MySQL**: A widely used open-source relational database management system.
- **PostgreSQL**: A powerful open-source RDBMS known for its advanced features and extensibility.
- **Oracle Database**: A commercial RDBMS with robust scalability and performance capabilities.
- **Microsoft SQL Server**: A popular commercial RDBMS by Microsoft, often used in enterprise applications.
- **SQLite**: As mentioned earlier, SQLite is a lightweight, serverless, and embedded RDBMS.

## Using Python Libraries for Database Connection

To connect to a relational database using Python, you typically need to install the appropriate database driver or library for your RDBMS. Here are some commonly used Python libraries for connecting to relational databases:

- **mysql-connector-python**: A Python driver for MySQL databases.
- **psycopg2**: A PostgreSQL adapter for Python.
- **cx_Oracle**: A Python extension module that allows access to Oracle databases.

- **pyodbc**: A Python module that provides access to Microsoft SQL Server databases.

## Example: Connecting to a PostgreSQL Database

Let's take a look at how to connect to a PostgreSQL database using the psycopg2 library:

```
import psycopg2

# Define the database connection parameters

db_params = {

'host': 'localhost',

'database': 'mydatabase',

'user': 'myuser',

'password': 'mypassword'

}

# Establish a connection to the database

connection = psycopg2.connect(**db_params)

# Create a cursor to execute SQL queries

cursor = connection.cursor()

# Execute SQL queries here...

# Commit changes and close the connection

connection.commit()

connection.close()
```

In this example, you specify the database connection parameters, establish a connection, create a cursor, execute SQL queries, and finally commit changes and close the connection.

### Conclusion

Python provides a wealth of libraries and modules that allow you to connect to various relational databases, making it a versatile choice for database interaction. Whether you're working with MySQL, PostgreSQL, Oracle, SQL Server, or other RDBMS systems, Python offers the tools you need to connect, query, and manage data effectively. In the next sections, we will explore more advanced topics related to working with databases, including NoSQL databases, web scraping, and data serialization.

## Section 7.4: NoSQL Databases and Python

In addition to relational databases, there is a growing demand for NoSQL (Not Only SQL) databases in the world of software development. NoSQL databases are designed to handle large volumes of unstructured or semi-structured data and are often used for applications where flexibility, scalability, and speed are paramount. In this section, we'll explore NoSQL databases and how to interact with them using Python.

### What Are NoSQL Databases?

NoSQL databases are a category of database management systems that depart from the traditional relational database model. They are characterized by their ability to store and manage vast amounts of data in various formats, including JSON, XML, key-value pairs, document stores, and graph databases. NoSQL databases are often chosen for projects where:

1. **Scalability**: NoSQL databases can scale horizontally, making them suitable for applications with unpredictable or rapidly growing datasets.
2. **Schema Flexibility**: NoSQL databases are schema-less or have flexible schemas, allowing you to change data structures on the fly.
3. **High Performance**: NoSQL databases are optimized for read and write operations in scenarios with high traffic and concurrent access.
4. **Complex Data Relationships**: For applications with complex, nested, or hierarchical data structures, document-oriented NoSQL databases are a good fit.

## Types of NoSQL Databases

There are several types of NoSQL databases, each designed to address specific use cases:

1. **Document Stores**: These databases store semi-structured data in documents, typically in formats like JSON or XML. Examples include MongoDB and CouchDB.
2. **Key-Value Stores**: Key-value stores are optimized for simple data storage and retrieval based on unique keys. Examples include Redis and Amazon DynamoDB.
3. **Column-Family Stores**: These databases are designed for handling large volumes of data and are often used in big data applications. Examples include Apache Cassandra and HBase.
4. **Graph Databases**: Graph databases are used for managing data with complex relationships. Examples include Neo4j and Amazon Neptune.

## Python Libraries for NoSQL Databases

Python provides libraries and drivers to interact with various NoSQL databases. Here are a few examples:

- **PyMongo**: A Python driver for MongoDB, a popular document-oriented NoSQL database.
- **redis-py**: A Python client for Redis, a high-performance key-value store.
- **cassandra-driver**: A Python driver for Apache Cassandra, a distributed column-family store.
- **py2neo**: A Python library for working with Neo4j, a graph database.

## Example: Using PyMongo with MongoDB

Let's take a quick look at how to use PyMongo to connect to a MongoDB database:

```
from pymongo import MongoClient

# Connect to the MongoDB server

client = MongoClient("mongodb://localhost:27017/")

# Access a specific database

db = client["mydatabase"]

# Access a collection (similar to a table in SQL)

collection = db["mycollection"]

# Insert a document into the collection
```

```
data = {"name": "John", "age": 30}

inserted_id = collection.insert_one(data).inserted_id

# Query data from the collection

result = collection.find_one({"_id": inserted_id})

print(result)

# Close the MongoDB connection

client.close()
```

In this example, we connect to a MongoDB database, insert a document into a collection, query data, and close the connection.

## Conclusion

NoSQL databases are an important part of the modern data landscape, offering flexible and scalable solutions for various data storage needs. Python provides libraries and drivers that allow you to connect to and interact with NoSQL databases efficiently. Whether you're working with document stores, key-value stores, column-family stores, or graph databases, Python has you covered for NoSQL database interaction. In the following sections, we will explore other aspects of Python libraries, including web scraping, data serialization, and machine learning.

# Section 7.5: Best Practices for Database Access

When working with databases in Python, it's important to follow best practices to ensure efficient and secure database access. In this section, we'll discuss some key best practices for database interaction using Python.

## 1. Use Prepared Statements

Prepared statements (or parameterized queries) are essential for preventing SQL injection attacks. Instead of embedding user input directly into SQL queries, use placeholders and bind variables to ensure that user input is treated as data and not executable code.

```
# Bad practice (vulnerable to SQL injection)

user_input = "'; DROP TABLE users;"

query = f"SELECT * FROM users WHERE username = '{user_input}'"

# Good practice (using prepared statement)

user_input = "'; DROP TABLE users;"

query = "SELECT * FROM users WHERE username = %s"

cursor.execute(query, (user_input,))
```

## 2. Close Database Connections

Always close database connections and cursors when you're done with them. Failing to do so can lead to resource leaks and performance issues.

```
# Bad practice (not closing the connection)

connection = psycopg2.connect(...)

# ...

# Do database operations

# ...
```

```
# Connection is not closed

# Good practice (closing the connection)

connection = psycopg2.connect(...)

# ...

# Do database operations

# ...

connection.close()
```

## 3. Use Connection Pools

For applications with high concurrency, consider using connection pooling libraries like psycopg2.pool or third-party libraries like SQLAlchemy with built-in connection pooling. Connection pooling helps manage database connections efficiently, reducing overhead.

```
from psycopg2 import pool

connection_pool = pool.SimpleConnectionPool(1, 10, ...)

connection = connection_pool.getconn()

# ...

# Use the connection

# ...

connection_pool.putconn(connection)
```

## 4. Handle Exceptions Gracefully

Database operations can fail due to various reasons, such as network issues or query errors. Always use try-except blocks to handle exceptions gracefully and provide meaningful error messages or log them for debugging.

```
try:
cursor.execute(query, params)
except psycopg2.Error as e:
print(f"Error executing query: {e}")
```

## 5. Implement Data Validation

Before inserting or updating data in the database, validate user input to ensure it meets the expected format and constraints. This helps prevent invalid data from entering the database.

```
def validate_user_input(user_input):
# Implement validation logic here
if len(user_input) < 5:
raise ValueError("Input is too short")
# Validate user input before database operation
try:
validate_user_input(user_input)
cursor.execute(query, params)
except ValueError as e:
```

print(f"Validation error: {e}")

## 6. Monitor and Optimize Queries

Regularly monitor database query performance using database profiling tools. Identify slow queries and optimize them by adding indexes, restructuring queries, or caching results where applicable.

## 7. Secure Database Credentials

Store database credentials securely, preferably in environment variables or configuration files, and avoid hardcoding credentials in your source code. Use encryption and access control mechanisms to protect sensitive data.

**import os DB_HOST = os.environ.get("DB_HOST") DB_PORT = os.environ.get("DB_PORT") DB_**

# Chapter 8: Web Scraping and API Integration

## Section 8.1: Basics of Web Scraping

Web scraping is the process of extracting data from websites. It allows you to retrieve information from web pages, whether it's text, images, or structured data, and use it for various purposes such as data analysis, research, or building applications. In this section, we will explore the basics of web scraping using Python.

### Why Web Scraping?

Web scraping can be a valuable tool for many tasks:

1. **Data Collection**: You can collect data from websites for research, analysis, or creating datasets.
2. **Competitive Analysis**: Monitor competitors' prices, products, or content.
3. **Content Aggregation**: Aggregate news articles, blog posts, or product listings.
4. **Automation**: Automate repetitive tasks like form filling or data extraction.

### Web Scraping Tools in Python

Python offers several libraries and frameworks for web scraping. Some popular choices include:

- **Beautiful Soup**: A library for parsing HTML and XML documents and extracting data.

- **Scrapy**: An open-source web crawling framework that simplifies the process of extracting data from websites.

- **Requests**: A Python library for making HTTP requests to retrieve web pages.

## Basic Web Scraping with Requests and Beautiful Soup

Let's see a simple example of how to use the requests library to fetch a web page's HTML content and BeautifulSoup to parse and extract data from it:

```
import requests

from bs4 import BeautifulSoup

# Send an HTTP GET request to the URL

url = "https://example.com"

response = requests.get(url)

# Check if the request was successful (status code 200)

if response.status_code == 200:

# Parse the HTML content of the page

soup = BeautifulSoup(response.text, "html.parser")

# Extract data

title = soup.title.text

first_paragraph = soup.find("p").text

print(f"Title: {title}")
```

```
print(f"First Paragraph: {first_paragraph}")
else:
print(f"Failed to retrieve the page (Status Code: {response.status_code})")
```

In this example, we send an HTTP GET request to a URL, check if the request is successful, parse the HTML content using Beautiful Soup, and extract the page's title and the text from the first paragraph.

### Ethical Considerations

When web scraping, it's essential to respect websites' terms of service and policies. Some websites may prohibit or limit scraping, so always review a site's robots.txt file and terms of use. Additionally, avoid overloading a website's server with too many requests, as this can impact its performance and result in IP bans.

### Conclusion

Web scraping is a powerful technique for extracting data from websites. Python offers libraries like Beautiful Soup, Scrapy, and Requests that make web scraping accessible and efficient. In the upcoming sections, we will delve deeper into web scraping techniques, parsing HTML and XML, handling dynamic content, and working with APIs to retrieve data programmatically.

## Section 8.2: BeautifulSoup for Parsing HTML

Beautiful Soup is a Python library that makes parsing HTML and XML documents easy and efficient. It provides tools for navigating and searching the parse tree, which is useful for web scraping and data extraction tasks. In this section, we will explore how to use BeautifulSoup for parsing HTML.

## Installing BeautifulSoup

You can install BeautifulSoup using pip:

```
pip install beautifulsoup4
```

## Parsing HTML

To parse an HTML document with BeautifulSoup, you typically start by creating a BeautifulSoup object from the HTML content. Here's a basic example:

```
from bs4 import BeautifulSoup

html_doc = """

<html>

<head>

<title>Sample Page</title>

</head>

<body>

<h1>Heading 1</h1>

<p>Paragraph 1</p>

<p>Paragraph 2</p>

</body>

</html>
```

```
"""

# Create a BeautifulSoup object

soup = BeautifulSoup(html_doc, 'html.parser')

# Access elements

title = soup.title

h1 = soup.h1

paragraphs = soup.find_all('p')

print(f"Title: {title.text}")

print(f"H1: {h1.text}")

for i, p in enumerate(paragraphs, 1):

print(f"Paragraph {i}: {p.text}")
```

In this example, we create a BeautifulSoup object called soup from the HTML content. We then access elements like the title, heading (<h1>), and paragraphs (<p>) within the HTML and print their text content.

## Navigating the Parse Tree

Beautiful Soup provides methods for navigating the parse tree. For example:

- find(): Finds the first matching element.
- find_all(): Finds all matching elements.
- parent(): Returns the parent element.

- children(): Returns a generator of a tag's children.
- next_sibling(): Returns the next sibling element.

### Searching by CSS Selectors

You can also use CSS selectors to find elements in the HTML:

```
# Find all <a> elements with class "link"

links = soup.select('a.link')

# Find the first <p> element inside a <div> with id "content"

paragraph = soup.select_one('div#content > p')
```

### Handling Dynamic Content

Beautiful Soup is excellent for static HTML parsing, but it may not handle dynamic web pages with JavaScript-generated content. In such cases, you may need to use a headless browser automation tool like Selenium.

### Conclusion

Beautiful Soup is a powerful library for parsing and navigating HTML and XML documents in Python. It simplifies the process of extracting data from web pages and is widely used in web scraping and data extraction tasks. In the next sections, we will explore more advanced web scraping techniques and tackle challenges such as handling AJAX-loaded content and scraping multiple pages.

## Section 8.3: Scrapy for Web Crawling

Scrapy is an open-source web crawling framework for Python that provides a more structured and powerful way to scrape data from websites. While Beautiful Soup is excellent for parsing HTML content, Scrapy takes web scraping to the next level by allowing you to build web crawlers that can navigate multiple pages, follow links, and extract data at scale. In this section, we will explore the basics of Scrapy and how to use it for web crawling.

## Installing Scrapy

You can install Scrapy using pip:

```
pip install scrapy
```

## Creating a Scrapy Project

To start using Scrapy, you need to create a Scrapy project. Use the following command:

```
scrapy startproject project_name
```

This will create a project directory structure with the necessary files and folders.

## Writing a Scrapy Spider

In Scrapy, a spider is a Python class that defines how to navigate and scrape a website. You can create a spider by running the following command inside your project directory:

```
scrapy genspider spider_name domain.com
```

This will generate a spider file where you can define the crawling behavior.

Here's a simple example of a Scrapy spider that extracts quotes from http://quotes.toscrape.com:

```
import scrapy
```

```
class QuotesSpider(scrapy.Spider):
name = "quotes"
start_urls = [
'http://quotes.toscrape.com/page/1/',
]
def parse(self, response):
for quote in response.css('div.quote'):
yield {
'text': quote.css('span.text::text').get(),
'author': quote.css('span small::text').get(),
}
next_page = response.css('li.next a::attr(href)').get()
if next_page is not None:
yield response.follow(next_page, self.parse)
```

In this example, the spider starts at the specified URL, extracts quotes and authors, and follows the link to the next page to continue scraping.

## Running a Scrapy Spider

To run a Scrapy spider, use the following command:

```
scrapy crawl spider_name
```

### Scrapy Features

Scrapy provides many features, including:

- **Middleware**: Customize the behavior of requests and responses.
- **Pipeline**: Process scraped data before storing it.
- **Item**: Define the structure of scraped data.
- **Settings**: Configure Scrapy's behavior.
- **Logging**: Debug and monitor the scraping process.

### Conclusion

Scrapy is a powerful web crawling framework for Python that simplifies the process of building web scrapers and crawlers. It is widely used for scraping and crawling websites to extract valuable data for various purposes, including data analysis, research, and content aggregation. In the next sections, we will explore more advanced Scrapy techniques and best practices for web crawling.

## Section 8.4: Working with RESTful APIs

In web scraping and data integration, you often encounter situations where you need to retrieve data from web services or APIs (Application Programming Interfaces). RESTful APIs, in particular, are a common way to access data from web servers. In this section, we will explore how to work with RESTful APIs in Python for data retrieval and integration.

## What is a RESTful API?

A RESTful API (Representational State Transfer API) is an architectural style for designing networked applications. It uses HTTP methods (GET, POST, PUT, DELETE) to perform CRUD (Create, Read, Update, Delete) operations on resources represented as URLs. RESTful APIs are widely used because they are simple, scalable, and can work over HTTP.

## Making GET Requests with requests

The requests library in Python simplifies the process of making HTTP requests, including GET requests to retrieve data from RESTful APIs. Here's an example of how to make a GET request to an API:

```
import requests

url = "https://api.example.com/data"

response = requests.get(url)

if response.status_code == 200:

data = response.json() # Parse the JSON response

print(data)

else:

print(f"Failed to retrieve data (Status Code: {response.status_code})")
```

In this example, we send a GET request to a URL and parse the JSON response. Many RESTful APIs return data in JSON format because it's human-readable and easy to work with in Python.

## Authenticating with APIs

Some APIs require authentication to access protected resources. You can include authentication credentials in your requests. For example, using an API key:

```
import requests

api_key = "your_api_key"

url = f"https://api.example.com/data?key={api_key}"

response = requests.get(url)

# Continue with handling the response
```

## Handling Pagination

When working with APIs that return paginated data, you may need to make multiple requests to retrieve all the data. Typically, the API will provide a way to specify the page number or offset in the request parameters.

## Rate Limiting and Throttling

Many APIs have rate limits to prevent abuse. Be sure to review the API's documentation to understand its rate limiting policies and handle rate limiting in your code.

## Error Handling

When working with APIs, it's essential to handle errors gracefully. Check the response status code and handle potential errors like rate limiting, authentication failures, or resource not found.

## Conclusion

Working with RESTful APIs is a crucial skill for data retrieval and integration in Python. The requests library simplifies making HTTP requests, and understanding the API's documentation is essential for successful data retrieval. In the next sections, we will explore more advanced API integration topics, including POST requests, authentication methods, and data transformation.

# Section 8.5: Handling Authentication and Rate Limiting

When working with web scraping and API integration, you may encounter the need to handle authentication and rate limiting. These considerations are essential for ensuring the smooth and ethical operation of your data retrieval processes. In this section, we will explore how to manage authentication and rate limiting in Python.

## Authentication Methods

### *API Keys*

API keys are a common method of authentication. When using an API that requires authentication, you typically obtain an API key from the service provider. Here's an example of how to include an API key in an HTTP request using the requests library:

```
import requests

api_key = "your_api_key"

url = f"https://api.example.com/data?key={api_key}"

response = requests.get(url)
```

*# Continue with handling the response*

### *OAuth 2.0*

OAuth 2.0 is a more secure authentication protocol used by many APIs. It involves obtaining access tokens to access protected resources on behalf of a user or an application. Libraries like oauthlib and requests-oauthlib can simplify OAuth 2.0 authentication.

## Rate Limiting

Rate limiting is a mechanism used by APIs to control the number of requests a client can make within a specified time period. Understanding and respecting rate limits is crucial to avoid being banned or restricted from an API.

### *Handling Rate Limits*

To handle rate limiting, you can implement logic in your code that respects the API's rate limit rules. Here's a simple example of how you can wait before making additional requests to comply with rate limits:

```
import requests

import time

def make_request_with_rate_limit(url, max_requests_per_minute):

current_minute = int(time.time()) // 60

if current_minute != make_request_with_rate_limit.last_minute:

make_request_with_rate_limit.requests_this_minute = 0
```

```
make_request_with_rate_limit.last_minute = current_minute

if make_request_with_rate_limit.requests_this_minute >= max_requests_per_minute:

# Wait for the next minute

time.sleep(60 - (int(time.time()) % 60))

response = requests.get(url)

make_request_with_rate_limit.requests_this_minute += 1

return response

make_request_with_rate_limit.last_minute = 0

make_request_with_rate_limit.requests_this_minute = 0
```

In this example, the make_request_with_rate_limit function checks if the number of requests made in the current minute exceeds the rate limit. If it does, it waits until the next minute to make another request.

## Conclusion

Handling authentication and rate limiting is essential when working with web scraping and APIs. Properly implementing authentication methods and rate limit handling in your code ensures that you can access and retrieve data without violating the service provider's policies. Additionally, it helps maintain a positive relationship with the API provider and ensures the longevity of your data integration processes.

# Chapter 9: Data Serialization and Formats

Serialization is the process of converting complex data structures, such as Python objects, into a format that can be easily stored, transmitted, and reconstructed. Deserialization is the reverse process, where the serialized data is converted back into its original form. Data serialization is essential in various scenarios, including data storage, communication between systems, and data exchange between different programming languages. In this chapter, we will explore different data serialization formats and how to work with them in Python.

## Section 9.1: Introduction to Data Serialization

### What is Data Serialization?

Data serialization is the process of converting data into a specific format so that it can be easily stored or transmitted and later reconstructed into its original form. Serialization is used in various applications, such as data storage, network communication, and inter-process communication.

Serialization is particularly crucial when data needs to be exchanged between different systems or programming languages. By serializing data into a standard format, you can ensure that data can be understood and processed correctly by different systems.

### Why Use Data Serialization?

There are several reasons to use data serialization:

1. **Data Persistence**: Serialization allows you to save the state of an object to a file or database. Later, you can deserialize the data to recreate the object's state.
2. **Data Exchange**: When different systems or applications need to communicate, they often use serialized data as a common format. This ensures compatibility and reduces the risk of data corruption.
3. **Cross-Language Communication**: Serialization enables communication between systems implemented in different programming languages. As long as both sides understand the serialization format, data can be exchanged seamlessly.

## Common Data Serialization Formats

Python supports various data serialization formats, each with its advantages and use cases. Some common serialization formats include:

- **JSON (JavaScript Object Notation)**: A lightweight text-based format commonly used for data exchange between web applications. It is human-readable and easy to work with in Python.

- **XML (eXtensible Markup Language)**: A markup language often used for structured data exchange. XML is more verbose than JSON but provides a well-defined schema.

- **YAML (YAML Ain't Markup Language)**: A human-readable data serialization format that is often used for configuration files.

- **Protocol Buffers (protobuf)**: A binary serialization format developed by Google. It is highly efficient and suitable for high-performance applications.

- **MessagePack**: A binary serialization format that is more compact and faster to serialize/deserialize than JSON.

In the following sections, we will delve into each of these serialization formats, discuss their usage, and demonstrate how to work with them in Python.

## Conclusion

Data serialization is a fundamental concept in software development, enabling data to be stored, exchanged, and processed efficiently. Understanding different serialization formats and knowing how to work with them in Python is essential for building robust and interoperable applications. In the subsequent sections of this chapter, we will explore specific serialization formats and how to use them effectively in Python.

# Section 9.2: Working with JSON

JSON (JavaScript Object Notation) is a lightweight data interchange format that is easy for humans to read and write and easy for machines to parse and generate. It has become one of the most common data formats used for web APIs, configuration files, and data storage. In this section, we will explore how to work with JSON in Python.

## JSON Basics

JSON represents data as key-value pairs and supports various data types, including strings, numbers, booleans, arrays, and nested objects. Here's a basic example of JSON data:

```
{
"name": "John Doe",
"age": 30,
"is_student": false,
"hobbies": ["reading", "gaming", "traveling"],
"address": {
"street": "123 Main St",
"city": "Anytown",
"state": "CA"
}
}
```

In Python, the json module is used to work with JSON data. You can convert between Python objects and JSON data using the json.dumps() method to serialize Python objects to JSON and json.loads() to deserialize JSON data into Python objects.

## Serializing Python Objects to JSON

To serialize a Python object to JSON, you can use the json.dumps() function. Here's an example:

```
import json

data = {

"name": "John Doe",

"age": 30,

"is_student": False,

"hobbies": ["reading", "gaming", "traveling"],

"address": {

"street": "123 Main St",

"city": "Anytown",

"state": "CA"

}

}

# Serialize the Python dictionary to JSON

json_data = json.dumps(data, indent=2) # Use indent for pretty-printing

print(json_data)
```

The indent parameter is used to specify the number of spaces for formatting the JSON output for better readability.

## Deserializing JSON into Python Objects

To deserialize JSON data into Python objects, you can use the json.loads() function. Here's an example:

```
import json
json_data = '''
{
"name": "John Doe",
"age": 30,
"is_student": false,
"hobbies": ["reading", "gaming", "traveling"],
"address": {
"street": "123 Main St",
"city": "Anytown",
"state": "CA"
}
}
'''
# Deserialize JSON data into a Python dictionary
data = json.loads(json_data)
print(data["name"]) # Accessing values from the Python dictionary
```

## Working with JSON Files

JSON data is often stored in files. To read JSON data from a file and write JSON data to a file, you can use the json.dump() and json.load() functions. Here's an example:

```
import json
data = {
"name": "John Doe",
"age": 30,
"is_student": False,
"hobbies": ["reading", "gaming", "traveling"],
"address": {
"street": "123 Main St",
"city": "Anytown",
"state": "CA"
}
}
# Write JSON data to a file
with open("data.json", "w") as json_file:
json.dump(data, json_file, indent=2)
# Read JSON data from a file
with open("data.json", "r") as json_file:
loaded_data = json.load(json_file)
print(loaded_data["name"])
```

## Conclusion

JSON is a versatile and widely used data serialization format in Python and many other programming languages. It provides a convenient way to represent structured data, making it suitable for various applications such as web APIs, configuration files, and data interchange. By using the json module in Python, you can easily work with JSON data, both for serializing Python objects to JSON and deserializing JSON into Python objects. In the next sections, we will explore other data serialization formats and their usage in Python.

# Section 9.3: XML and HTML Parsing

XML (eXtensible Markup Language) and HTML (Hypertext Markup Language) are both markup languages used for structuring and presenting data. While HTML is primarily used for web page content, XML is more versatile and can represent structured data in various domains. In this section, we will explore how to parse XML and HTML documents in Python.

## Parsing XML with ElementTree

Python provides the ElementTree module as a standard library for parsing XML documents. It allows you to parse XML data and navigate the XML tree structure easily. Here's a basic example of parsing an XML document:

```
import xml.etree.ElementTree as ET

# Sample XML data

xml_data = '''

<bookstore>
```

```
<book>
<title>Python Programming</title>
<author>John Doe</author>
<price>29.95</price>
</book>
<book>
<title>Data Science with Python</title>
<author>Jane Smith</author>
<price>39.99</price>
</book>
</bookstore>
'''
# Parse the XML data
root = ET.fromstring(xml_data)
# Access elements and attributes
for book in root.findall("book"):
title = book.find("title").text
author = book.find("author").text
price = book.find("price").text
print(f"Title: {title}, Author: {author}, Price: ${price}")
```

## Parsing HTML with BeautifulSoup

To parse HTML documents in Python, the BeautifulSoup library is widely used. It provides a convenient way to navigate and manipulate HTML content. Here's an example of parsing an HTML document:

```
from bs4 import BeautifulSoup

# Sample HTML data

html_data = '''

<html>

<body>

<h1>Welcome to My Website</h1>

<p>This is a paragraph.</p>

<ul>

<li>Item 1</li>

<li>Item 2</li>

<li>Item 3</li>

</ul>

</body>

</html>

'''

# Parse the HTML data

soup = BeautifulSoup(html_data, "html.parser")
```

```
# Access elements and content

heading = soup.h1.text

paragraph = soup.p.text

items = [li.text for li in soup.find_all("li")]

print(f"Heading: {heading}")

print(f"Paragraph: {paragraph}")

print(f"List Items: {', '.join(items)}")
```

## HTML Parsing with Requests and BeautifulSoup

Often, you need to parse HTML from web pages. You can use the requests library to fetch web content and then parse it with BeautifulSoup. Here's an example:

```
import requests

from bs4 import BeautifulSoup

# Send an HTTP request and get the web page content

url = "https://example.com"

response = requests.get(url)

# Parse the HTML content

soup = BeautifulSoup(response.text, "html.parser")

# Access elements and content as shown in the previous example
```

## Conclusion

XML and HTML parsing are essential tasks in web development and data processing. Python provides libraries like ElementTree for XML parsing and BeautifulSoup for HTML parsing, making it easy to work with structured data from various sources. Whether you're dealing with XML-based configuration files or scraping data from web pages, these tools are invaluable for extracting information from markup languages. In the following sections, we will explore other data serialization formats and parsing techniques in Python.

# Section 9.4: YAML and Other Serialization Formats

YAML (YAML Ain't Markup Language) is a human-readable data serialization format often used for configuration files and data exchange between languages with different data structures. It is designed to be easy for humans to read and write, making it a popular choice for configuration files in software projects.

## Working with YAML in Python

Python has a library called PyYAML that allows you to work with YAML data easily. You can install it using pip:

```
pip install pyyaml
```

Here's a basic example of working with YAML in Python:

```
import yaml

# Sample YAML data

yaml_data = """

name: John Doe
```

```
age: 30

email: johndoe@example.com

"""

# Parse YAML data

data = yaml.safe_load(yaml_data)

# Access values

name = data["name"]

age = data["age"]

email = data["email"]

print(f"Name: {name}, Age: {age}, Email: {email}")
```

## Other Serialization Formats

Besides JSON, XML, and YAML, there are other serialization formats you might encounter:

1. **CSV (Comma-Separated Values):** CSV files are often used for tabular data. Python's csv module provides functionalities for reading and writing CSV files.
2. **INI:** INI files are used for configuration settings and are organized into sections and key-value pairs. Python's configparser module can parse and manipulate INI files.
3. **TOML (Tom's Obvious, Minimal Language):** TOML is a configuration file format that aims to be easy to read due to its simple syntax. The tomli library allows Python to work with TOML data.
4. **MessagePack:** MessagePack is a binary serialization format

that is more compact and efficient than JSON. The msgpack library enables Python to encode and decode MessagePack data.

5. **HJSON (Human JSON):** HJSON is a JSON extension with a more lenient syntax, allowing comments and relaxed quoting rules. The hjson library can be used for HJSON in Python.

When working with these formats, it's essential to use the appropriate libraries and tools for parsing and serializing data effectively. Python's ecosystem provides various libraries to handle different serialization formats, making it versatile for data processing tasks.

## Section 9.5: Protocol Buffers and Avro

Protocol Buffers (protobuf) and Avro are binary serialization formats that focus on efficiency and language-agnostic data interchange. They are often used in distributed systems, where compact and fast serialization is crucial.

### Protocol Buffers (protobuf)

Protocol Buffers, developed by Google, are a widely used binary serialization format. It offers a schema definition language for specifying data structures, and it generates code in various programming languages for data serialization and deserialization. Here's a brief overview of how protobuf works in Python:

1. **Define a .proto File:** Start by creating a .proto file that defines your data structure using the protobuf schema language. Here's an example:

```
syntax = "proto3";

message Person {

string name = 1;

int32 age = 2;

}
```

1. **Compile the .proto File:** Use the protoc compiler to generate Python code from the .proto file:

```
protoc—python_out=. your_file.proto
```

1. **Serialize and Deserialize Data:** Now, you can use the generated Python code to serialize and deserialize data:

```
import your_file_pb2

# Create a Person object

person = your_file_pb2.Person()

person.name = "John"

person.age = 30

# Serialize to bytes

serialized_data = person.SerializeToString()

# Deserialize from bytes

new_person = your_file_pb2.Person()

new_person.ParseFromString(serialized_data)
```

```
print(f"Name: {new_person.name}, Age: {new_person.age}")
```

Protocol Buffers are efficient in terms of both space and time, making them a good choice for scenarios with high-performance requirements.

## Avro

Apache Avro is another binary serialization format designed for data exchange in distributed systems. Avro also uses schemas to define data structures and supports schema evolution. Here's a basic introduction to Avro in Python:

1. **Define an Avro Schema:** Create an Avro schema in JSON format to specify your data structure. Here's an example schema for a user:

```
{
"type": "record",
"name": "User",
"fields": [
{"name": "name", "type": "string"},
{"name": "age", "type": "int"}
]
}
```

1. **Serialize and Deserialize Data:** Use the fastavro library to work with Avro data:

```
import fastavro

# Define the Avro schema

schema = {

"type": "record",

"name": "User",

"fields": [

{"name": "name", "type": "string"},

{"name": "age", "type": "int"}

]

}

# Create a User object

user = {"name": "Alice", "age": 25}

# Serialize to Avro binary

avro_data = fastavro.schemaless_writer(user, schema)

# Deserialize from Avro binary

deserialized_user = fastavro.parse_schemaless(avro_data, schema)

print(f"Name: {deserialized_user['name']}, Age: {deserialized_user['age']}")
```

Avro's support for schema evolution makes it suitable for systems where data schemas may change over time without breaking compatibility.

In summary, Protocol Buffers and Avro are efficient binary serialization formats that offer schema definition, language independence, and support for high-performance data serialization and deserialization. Depending on your specific use case and requirements, you can choose one of these formats for efficient data exchange in your applications.

# Chapter 10: Machine Learning with scikit-learn

## Section 10.1: Introduction to Machine Learning in Python

Machine learning is a subfield of artificial intelligence that focuses on developing algorithms and models that enable computers to learn from and make predictions or decisions based on data. In Python, scikit-learn (or sklearn) is one of the most popular libraries for machine learning tasks. It provides a wide range of tools and algorithms for tasks such as classification, regression, clustering, dimensionality reduction, and more.

### Key Concepts in Machine Learning

Before diving into scikit-learn, it's essential to understand some fundamental concepts in machine learning:

1. **Data:** Machine learning relies on data. You need a dataset that contains features (input variables) and labels (output or target variable). The quality and quantity of data play a crucial role in model performance.
2. **Features:** Features are the attributes or characteristics of your data that you use as input for your machine learning model. Feature engineering is the process of selecting, transforming, or creating features to improve model accuracy.
3. **Labels:** Labels are the target variables you want your model to predict. In supervised learning, you have labeled data, meaning each data point has a corresponding label. In unsupervised learning, there are no labels, and the

algorithm identifies patterns or groups in the data.

4. **Model:** A machine learning model is a mathematical representation of a real-world process. It learns from the data during the training phase and makes predictions or decisions during the inference phase.
5. **Training and Testing:** To evaluate a machine learning model, you typically split your dataset into two parts: a training set and a testing set. The model learns from the training set and is evaluated on the testing set to measure its performance.
6. **Supervised vs. Unsupervised Learning:** In supervised learning, the model is trained on labeled data to make predictions. In unsupervised learning, the model identifies patterns or groups in the data without labeled examples.

## scikit-learn: Your Swiss Army Knife for ML

scikit-learn provides a unified interface for various machine learning algorithms and tasks. Here's a high-level overview of what scikit-learn offers:

- **Supervised Learning Algorithms:** You can find implementations of popular supervised learning algorithms such as linear regression, support vector machines, decision trees, and random forests.

- **Unsupervised Learning Algorithms:** scikit-learn supports unsupervised learning tasks like clustering (K-Means, DBSCAN), dimensionality reduction (PCA, t-SNE), and anomaly detection.

- **Model Evaluation:** The library includes functions for model evaluation, cross-validation, and hyperparameter tuning to ensure your models perform optimally.

- **Data Preprocessing:** scikit-learn provides tools for data preprocessing, including feature scaling, encoding categorical variables, and handling missing data.

- **Model Selection:** You can compare and select the best model for your task using tools like grid search and cross-validation.

- **Integration with NumPy and pandas:** scikit-learn seamlessly integrates with popular data manipulation libraries like NumPy and pandas, making it easy to preprocess and feed data into your models.

- **Extensibility:** While scikit-learn offers a wide range of algorithms out of the box, you can also build custom transformers and models to fit your specific needs.

To get started with scikit-learn, you'll need a good understanding of Python programming, data preprocessing, and the machine learning concepts mentioned above. In the subsequent sections of this chapter, we'll explore various aspects of using scikit-learn to create and evaluate machine learning models.

## Section 10.2: scikit-learn Overview

Now that you have a fundamental understanding of machine learning concepts, let's dive into an overview of scikit-learn. Scikit-learn is a powerful Python library that simplifies the process of building, training, and evaluating machine learning models. In this section, we'll explore the key components and functionalities that scikit-learn offers.

## The Estimator API

Scikit-learn follows a consistent and intuitive design pattern called the "Estimator API." This API defines a set of rules and conventions that all scikit-learn models adhere to. The core principles of the Estimator API are as follows:

1. **Consistency:** All scikit-learn estimators (models) implement a consistent interface. This means that you can use the same methods and attributes regardless of the type of model you're working with.
2. **Consolidation of Parameters:** Model hyperparameters are set via constructor arguments when creating an instance of the estimator. This ensures that all parameters are explicitly specified.
3. **Data Transformation:** Scikit-learn includes transformers for data preprocessing. These transformers follow the same API as the models, making it easy to combine data preprocessing steps with model training.
4. **Fit-Predict Interface:** The primary methods are fit() for training a model and predict() for making predictions. This uniform interface simplifies the model training and prediction process.

## Commonly Used scikit-learn Modules

Scikit-learn is organized into several modules, each focusing on specific aspects of machine learning. Here are some of the commonly used modules:

1. **sklearn.datasets:** This module provides access to various

datasets for practice and experimentation. You can load datasets like the famous Iris dataset or the digits dataset for digit recognition.

2. **sklearn.model_selection:** This module contains functions for splitting datasets into training and testing sets, as well as performing cross-validation. It helps you assess your model's performance effectively.
3. **sklearn.preprocessing:** Data preprocessing is a crucial step in machine learning. This module offers tools for feature scaling, encoding categorical variables, and handling missing values.
4. **sklearn.feature_extraction:** If you're working with text data, this module provides methods for extracting features from text, including techniques like TF-IDF (Term Frequency-Inverse Document Frequency).
5. **sklearn.linear_model:** Linear models are fundamental in machine learning. This module contains implementations of linear regression, logistic regression, and other linear models.
6. **sklearn.ensemble:** Ensemble methods combine multiple models to improve predictive performance. You'll find popular ensemble techniques like Random Forests and Gradient Boosting here.
7. **sklearn.cluster:** Clustering is an unsupervised learning technique. This module includes algorithms for K-Means clustering, DBSCAN, and more.
8. **sklearn.metrics:** Model evaluation is essential. This module provides various metrics for assessing classification, regression, and clustering models.

## Workflow with scikit-learn

Typically, your workflow with scikit-learn involves the following steps:

1. **Data Preparation:** Load and preprocess your dataset. This includes feature engineering, handling missing values, and scaling features.
2. **Model Selection:** Choose the appropriate machine learning algorithm(s) for your task. Scikit-learn offers a wide range of models.
3. **Model Training:** Create an instance of the chosen model(s), set hyperparameters, and use the fit() method to train the model on your training data.
4. **Model Evaluation:** Use metrics and cross-validation techniques from the sklearn.metrics and sklearn.model_selection modules to evaluate your model's performance on a testing dataset.
5. **Hyperparameter Tuning:** Fine-tune your model by adjusting hyperparameters using techniques like grid search or randomized search.
6. **Model Deployment:** Once satisfied with your model's performance, you can deploy it to make predictions on new data.

In the upcoming sections of this chapter, we'll delve deeper into each of these steps and provide practical examples of using scikit-learn for various machine learning tasks.

## Section 10.3: Data Preprocessing with scikit-learn

Data preprocessing is a crucial step in the machine learning pipeline. It involves preparing and cleaning the dataset to ensure that it's in a suitable format for training machine learning models. Scikit-learn provides a wide range of tools and transformers to help you preprocess your data effectively.

### Data Scaling and Normalization

One common preprocessing step is scaling or normalizing the features in your dataset. Many machine learning algorithms perform better when features are on a similar scale. Scikit-learn provides the StandardScaler and MinMaxScaler transformers for this purpose.

Here's an example of how to use the StandardScaler to standardize your feature values:

```
from sklearn.preprocessing import StandardScaler

# Create a StandardScaler instance

scaler = StandardScaler()

# Fit the scaler to your training data and transform it

X_train_scaled = scaler.fit_transform(X_train)

# Use the same scaler to transform your testing data

X_test_scaled = scaler.transform(X_test)
```

### Handling Missing Data

Dealing with missing data is another essential preprocessing task. Scikit-learn provides the SimpleImputer transformer to fill in missing values with a chosen strategy, such as mean, median, or a constant value.

```
from sklearn.impute import SimpleImputer

# Create a SimpleImputer instance with the strategy to use (e.g., 'mean')

imputer = SimpleImputer(strategy='mean')

# Fit the imputer to your training data and transform it

X_train_imputed = imputer.fit_transform(X_train)

# Use the same imputer to transform your testing data

X_test_imputed = imputer.transform(X_test)
```

## Encoding Categorical Data

Many machine learning algorithms work with numerical data, so you often need to encode categorical variables. Scikit-learn provides the OneHotEncoder and LabelEncoder for this purpose.

```
from sklearn.preprocessing import OneHotEncoder, LabelEncoder

# Create a LabelEncoder instance for a single categorical feature

label_encoder = LabelEncoder()

# Fit and transform the label encoder on a categorical feature

X_train_encoded =
label_encoder.fit_transform(X_train['categorical_feature'])

# Use the same label encoder to transform your testing data

X_test_encoded =
label_encoder.transform(X_test['categorical_feature'])
```

*# Alternatively, use OneHotEncoder to convert categorical features into binary vectors*

encoder = OneHotEncoder(sparse=False)

*# Fit and transform the one-hot encoder on categorical features*

X_train_encoded = encoder.fit_transform(X_train[['categorical_feature']])

*# Use the same encoder to transform your testing data*

X_test_encoded = encoder.transform(X_test[['categorical_feature']])

## Feature Engineering

Sometimes, you might need to create new features from existing ones to improve model performance. Scikit-learn doesn't directly provide feature engineering tools, but you can use standard Python and NumPy operations to create new features based on your domain knowledge.

## Text Data Processing

If your dataset includes text data, scikit-learn offers several tools for text preprocessing, including text vectorization techniques like TF-IDF and word embeddings. You can use these techniques to convert text data into a numerical format that can be used by machine learning models.

**from** sklearn.feature_extraction.text **import** TfidfVectorizer

*# Create a TF-IDF vectorizer instance*

tfidf_vectorizer = TfidfVectorizer()

```
# Fit and transform the vectorizer on your text data

X_train_tfidf = tfidf_vectorizer.fit_transform(X_train_text)

# Use the same vectorizer to transform your testing text data

X_test_tfidf = tfidf_vectorizer.transform(X_test_text)
```

These are some of the essential data preprocessing techniques available in scikit-learn. Depending on your specific dataset and machine learning task, you may need to apply additional preprocessing steps such as feature selection, dimensionality reduction, or custom transformations. Scikit-learn's flexibility and extensive library of transformers make it a powerful tool for handling data preprocessing in machine learning projects.

## Section 10.4: Supervised Learning Algorithms

Supervised learning is one of the fundamental branches of machine learning, where the model learns from labeled data to make predictions or decisions. Scikit-learn offers a wide range of supervised learning algorithms for classification and regression tasks.

### Classification Algorithms

Classification is a type of supervised learning where the goal is to assign a label or category to input data. Scikit-learn provides various classification algorithms, including:

1. **Logistic Regression:** Despite its name, logistic regression is a classification algorithm used for binary and multi-class classification tasks.

```
from sklearn.linear_model import LogisticRegression
```

```
# Create a logistic regression classifier

classifier = LogisticRegression()

# Train the classifier on your training data

classifier.fit(X_train, y_train)

# Make predictions on new data

y_pred = classifier.predict(X_test)
```

1. **Decision Trees:** Decision trees are tree-like models that split data based on the features to make decisions.

```
from sklearn.tree import DecisionTreeClassifier

# Create a decision tree classifier

classifier = DecisionTreeClassifier()

# Train the classifier on your training data

classifier.fit(X_train, y_train)

# Make predictions on new data

y_pred = classifier.predict(X_test)
```

1. **Random Forests:** Random forests are an ensemble of decision trees, which can provide better generalization and accuracy.

```
from sklearn.ensemble import RandomForestClassifier

# Create a random forest classifier
```

```
classifier = RandomForestClassifier()

# Train the classifier on your training data

classifier.fit(X_train, y_train)

# Make predictions on new data

y_pred = classifier.predict(X_test)
```

1. **Support Vector Machines (SVM):** SVM is a powerful classification algorithm that finds the optimal hyperplane to separate classes.

```
from sklearn.svm import SVC

# Create an SVM classifier

classifier = SVC()

# Train the classifier on your training data

classifier.fit(X_train, y_train)

# Make predictions on new data

y_pred = classifier.predict(X_test)
```

1. **K-Nearest Neighbors (KNN):** KNN classifies data points based on the majority class among their k nearest neighbors.

```
from sklearn.neighbors import KNeighborsClassifier

# Create a KNN classifier with a specified number of neighbors (k)
```

```
classifier = KNeighborsClassifier(n_neighbors=5)

# Train the classifier on your training data

classifier.fit(X_train, y_train)

# Make predictions on new data

y_pred = classifier.predict(X_test)
```

## Regression Algorithms

Regression is another supervised learning task where the goal is to predict a continuous numeric value. Scikit-learn offers regression algorithms such as:

1. **Linear Regression:** Linear regression models the relationship between the input features and the target variable as a linear equation.

```
from sklearn.linear_model import LinearRegression

# Create a linear regression model

regressor = LinearRegression()

# Train the model on your training data

regressor.fit(X_train, y_train)

# Make predictions on new data

y_pred = regressor.predict(X_test)
```

1. **Decision Trees for Regression:** Decision trees can also be used for regression tasks by predicting the average target

value within each leaf node.

```
from sklearn.tree import DecisionTreeRegressor

# Create a decision tree regressor

regressor = DecisionTreeRegressor()

# Train the regressor on your training data

regressor.fit(X_train, y_train)

# Make predictions on new data

y_pred = regressor.predict(X_test)
```

1. **Random Forests for Regression:** Random forests can be used for regression tasks as well, providing robust predictions.

```
from sklearn.ensemble import RandomForestRegressor

# Create a random forest regressor

regressor = RandomForestRegressor()

# Train the regressor on your training data

regressor.fit(X_train, y_train)

# Make predictions on new data

y_pred = regressor.predict(X_test)
```

1. **Support Vector Machines for Regression (SVR):** SVR is a regression variant of the SVM algorithm.

```python
from sklearn.svm import SVR

# Create an SVR model

regressor = SVR()

# Train the model on your training data

regressor.fit(X_train, y_train)

# Make predictions on new data

y_pred = regressor.predict(X_test)
```

These are just a few examples of supervised learning algorithms available in scikit-learn. The choice of algorithm depends on the nature of your data and the specific problem you're trying to solve. It's essential to understand the characteristics of each algorithm and experiment with them to find the one that performs best for your particular task.

## Section 10.5: Unsupervised Learning Techniques

Unsupervised learning is a branch of machine learning where the model is trained on data without labeled outputs. The goal is to discover patterns, relationships, or structures within the data. Scikit-learn provides various unsupervised learning techniques, including clustering and dimensionality reduction.

### Clustering

Clustering is a common unsupervised learning technique used to group similar data points together. It's particularly useful for tasks like customer segmentation, image segmentation, and anomaly detection.

### *K-Means Clustering*

K-means is a popular clustering algorithm that partitions data into 'k' clusters based on the similarity of data points. Here's how you can use it:

```
from sklearn.cluster import KMeans

# Create a K-means clustering model with 'k' clusters

kmeans = KMeans(n_clusters=3)

# Fit the model to your data

kmeans.fit(X)

# Get cluster assignments for each data point

labels = kmeans.labels_

# Get the coordinates of cluster centers

cluster_centers = kmeans.cluster_centers_
```

### *Hierarchical Clustering*

Hierarchical clustering builds a tree-like structure of nested clusters, making it suitable for hierarchical data. It doesn't require specifying the number of clusters in advance.

```
from sklearn.cluster import AgglomerativeClustering

# Create a hierarchical clustering model
```

```
agg_clustering = AgglomerativeClustering(n_clusters=3)

# Fit the model to your data

agg_clustering.fit(X)

# Get cluster assignments for each data point

labels = agg_clustering.labels_
```

## Dimensionality Reduction

Dimensionality reduction techniques aim to reduce the number of features in a dataset while preserving essential information. This can help improve model efficiency and interpretability.

### *Principal Component Analysis (PCA)*

PCA is a widely used technique to reduce the dimensionality of data while retaining most of its variance.

```
from sklearn.decomposition import PCA

# Create a PCA model with a specified number of components

pca = PCA(n_components=2)

# Fit the model to your data and transform it

X_pca = pca.fit_transform(X)
```

### *t-Distributed Stochastic Neighbor Embedding (t-SNE)*

t-SNE is another dimensionality reduction technique, well-suited for visualizing high-dimensional data in a lower-dimensional space.

```
from sklearn.manifold import TSNE
```

```
# Create a t-SNE model with a specified number of dimensions

tsne = TSNE(n_components=2)

# Fit the model to your data and transform it

X_tsne = tsne.fit_transform(X)
```

These unsupervised learning techniques are valuable tools for exploring and understanding your data, especially when you don't have labeled targets. Clustering helps you discover natural groupings within your data, while dimensionality reduction can simplify complex datasets for visualization and analysis. The choice of technique depends on your specific problem and goals.

# Chapter 11: Deep Learning with TensorFlow and Keras

## Section 11.1: Deep Learning Fundamentals

Deep learning is a subfield of machine learning that has gained significant attention in recent years due to its remarkable success in various applications, including image and speech recognition, natural language processing, and autonomous driving. At its core, deep learning involves training artificial neural networks to perform tasks by learning from data. In this section, we'll delve into the fundamentals of deep learning and explore its key concepts.

### What is Deep Learning?

Deep learning refers to the training of neural networks with multiple layers, known as deep neural networks. These networks are designed to automatically learn patterns, features, and representations from raw data, making them capable of solving complex tasks that were once challenging for traditional machine learning algorithms.

At the heart of deep learning are artificial neurons, which are inspired by the biological neurons in the human brain. These neurons are organized into layers, typically consisting of an input layer, one or more hidden layers, and an output layer. The hidden layers are where most of the learning occurs as they transform the input data into more abstract representations.

### Artificial Neural Networks (ANNs)

Artificial neural networks (ANNs) are the building blocks of deep learning. An ANN is composed of interconnected artificial neurons, also known as nodes or units, which process and transmit information. Each connection between neurons has an associated weight, which determines the strength of the connection. The output of a neuron is calculated by applying an activation function to the weighted sum of its inputs.

## Training Neural Networks

The training process of a neural network involves adjusting the weights of its connections to minimize a loss or error function. This process is known as backpropagation and typically utilizes optimization techniques like stochastic gradient descent (SGD) to update the weights. During training, the network learns to make predictions that are as close as possible to the ground truth labels provided in the training data.

## Deep Learning Architectures

Deep learning encompasses a variety of neural network architectures tailored to different types of tasks. Convolutional Neural Networks (CNNs) excel in image recognition tasks by using convolutional layers to capture spatial patterns. Recurrent Neural Networks (RNNs) are designed for sequential data, making them suitable for tasks like natural language processing. Long Short-Term Memory (LSTM) networks and Gated Recurrent Unit (GRU) networks are specialized RNN variants that address the vanishing gradient problem.

## Deep Learning Frameworks

To implement deep learning models, practitioners often use deep learning frameworks like TensorFlow and Keras. TensorFlow is an open-source machine learning library developed by Google that provides a flexible platform for building and training neural networks. Keras is a high-level neural networks API that runs on top of TensorFlow (among other backends) and simplifies the process of defining and training deep learning models.

Deep learning has revolutionized various fields, enabling breakthroughs in computer vision, natural language processing, and reinforcement learning. In the subsequent sections of this chapter, we will explore practical aspects of deep learning, including how to work with TensorFlow and Keras to build and train neural networks for specific tasks.

## Section 11.2: Introduction to TensorFlow

TensorFlow is an open-source machine learning framework developed by Google that has become one of the most popular tools for building and training deep neural networks. In this section, we'll provide an introduction to TensorFlow and its key features.

### What is TensorFlow?

TensorFlow is designed to facilitate the development of machine learning models, particularly deep learning models, by providing a flexible and efficient framework. It is characterized by its ability to work with large datasets, perform distributed computing, and optimize the execution of neural networks on various hardware platforms, including CPUs and GPUs.

### Key Features of TensorFlow

1. **Computational Graph**: TensorFlow models are represented as computational graphs. In a computational graph, nodes represent mathematical operations, and edges represent the data (tensors) flowing between these operations. This graph-based approach enables efficient optimization and execution of operations.

2. **Automatic Differentiation**: TensorFlow has built-in support for automatic differentiation, a crucial component of training deep neural networks. It computes gradients with respect to model parameters, allowing for gradient-based optimization techniques like stochastic gradient descent.
3. **Flexible Deployment**: TensorFlow models can be deployed on various platforms, including desktops, servers, and mobile devices. TensorFlow Serving and TensorFlow Lite are tools that facilitate model deployment and inference.
4. **High-Level APIs**: TensorFlow provides high-level APIs, such as Keras, tf.keras, and Estimators, which simplify the process of building and training neural networks. Keras, in particular, is widely used for its user-friendly interface and seamless integration with TensorFlow.
5. **TensorBoard**: TensorFlow includes TensorBoard, a visualization tool that helps users visualize and monitor training progress, model architectures, and performance metrics. This aids in debugging and optimizing models.
6. **Ecosystem**: TensorFlow has a rich ecosystem of libraries and extensions for various tasks, including TensorFlow Extended (TFX) for production ML pipelines, TensorFlow Hub for reusable model components, and TensorFlow.js for machine learning in JavaScript.

## TensorFlow 2.x

TensorFlow 2.x is the latest version of the framework and represents a significant shift from TensorFlow 1.x. It introduces many improvements aimed at making TensorFlow more user-friendly and accessible. Some notable changes in TensorFlow 2.x include:

- **Eager Execution**: TensorFlow 2.x adopts eager execution by default, which makes it easier to debug models and work with TensorFlow in an imperative programming style similar to NumPy.

- **Simplified API**: The integration of Keras into TensorFlow as tf.keras simplifies model building and training, making it the recommended high-level API for most users.

- **Dynamic Computation Graphs**: While static computation graphs are still possible, TensorFlow 2.x allows dynamic computation graphs by default, eliminating the need for placeholders and sessions.

- **Better GPU Support**: TensorFlow 2.x improves GPU support, making it more seamless to leverage GPUs for accelerated training.

- **Compatibility**: TensorFlow 2.x is designed to be compatible with TensorFlow 1.x code, making it easier for users to transition to the new version.

In the upcoming sections, we will explore practical examples of using TensorFlow and Keras to build and train deep learning models for various tasks, including image classification and natural language processing.

## Section 11.3: Building Neural Networks with Keras

Keras is a high-level deep learning API that is integrated with TensorFlow (as tf.keras), making it a popular choice for building and training neural networks. In this section, we'll explore how to use

Keras to create and configure neural networks for various machine learning tasks.

## Key Concepts in Keras

### *1. Sequential Model*

In Keras, the Sequential model is a linear stack of layers, where you can easily add one layer at a time. This is the simplest way to create a neural network. Here's an example of creating a sequential model in Keras:

```
from tensorflow import keras

model = keras.Sequential()

model.add(keras.layers.Dense(64, activation='relu', input_shape=(784,)))

model.add(keras.layers.Dense(10, activation='softmax'))
```

In this example, we define a sequential model with two layers: a dense layer with 64 units and ReLU activation, followed by another dense layer with 10 units and softmax activation.

### *2. Functional API*

The functional API in Keras allows for more complex model architectures. It's suitable for creating models with multiple inputs, multiple outputs, and shared layers. Here's an example of defining a model using the functional API:

```
from tensorflow import keras

from tensorflow.keras.layers import Input, Dense
```

```
# Define input layer

input_layer = Input(shape=(784,))

# Define hidden layers

hidden_layer = Dense(64, activation='relu')(input_layer)

output_layer = Dense(10, activation='softmax')(hidden_layer)

# Create the model

model = keras.Model(inputs=input_layer, outputs=output_layer)
```

In this example, we create an input layer, define the hidden layers, and specify the output layer. Then, we create the model by specifying the input and output layers.

### *3. Model Compilation*

Before training a model, you need to compile it by specifying the loss function, optimizer, and evaluation metrics. Here's an example of compiling a model:

```
model.compile(optimizer='adam',

loss='sparse_categorical_crossentropy',

metrics=['accuracy'])
```

In this example, we compile the model with the Adam optimizer, sparse categorical cross-entropy loss (suitable for classification tasks), and accuracy as the evaluation metric.

### Training and Evaluation

Once the model is defined and compiled, you can train it using training data and evaluate its performance on test data. Here's a simplified example of the training process:

```
model.fit(train_images, train_labels, epochs=10, validation_data=(test_images, test_labels))
```

This code snippet trains the model for 10 epochs using the training data and validates it using the test data.

### Transfer Learning

Keras also supports transfer learning, which involves using pre-trained models as a starting point for your own tasks. You can fine-tune a pre-trained model by adding custom layers or retraining some of its layers on your specific dataset. This is particularly useful when you have limited data for your task.

In the next sections, we'll delve deeper into practical examples of using Keras for various machine learning and deep learning tasks, including image classification and text sentiment analysis. We'll explore more advanced concepts and best practices for building and training neural networks.

## Section 11.4: Training Deep Learning Models

Training deep learning models is a crucial step in utilizing neural networks for various machine learning tasks. In this section, we will delve into the details of training neural networks using Keras.

## Dataset Preparation

Before training a deep learning model, you need to prepare your dataset. It typically involves the following steps:

1. **Data Loading**: Load your dataset into memory. Keras provides utilities to load common datasets like MNIST, CIFAR-10, and more. For custom datasets, you'll need to load and preprocess the data yourself.
2. **Data Preprocessing**: Preprocess the data to make it suitable for training. This may include resizing images, normalizing pixel values, one-hot encoding labels, and splitting the data into training, validation, and test sets.
3. **Data Augmentation**: For computer vision tasks, data augmentation techniques like rotation, flipping, and scaling can be applied to artificially increase the size of the training dataset and improve model generalization.

## Model Training

Once your dataset is prepared, you can start training your deep learning model. Here's a high-level overview of the training process:

1. **Model Compilation**: As discussed in Section 11.3, you compile your model by specifying the loss function, optimizer, and evaluation metrics.
2. **Model Training**: Use the model.fit() method to train your model. This method takes the training data, validation data (optional), batch size, and the number of epochs as parameters. During training, the model's weights are adjusted to minimize the specified loss function.
3. **Monitoring Progress**: Keras provides callbacks that allow you to monitor and visualize training progress. You can use callbacks to save model checkpoints, log training metrics,

and stop training early if performance doesn't improve.

4. **Hyperparameter Tuning**: Experiment with different hyperparameters like learning rate, batch size, and network architecture to find the best combination for your specific task.
5. **Regularization**: Apply regularization techniques like dropout or L1/L2 regularization to prevent overfitting.
6. **Transfer Learning**: For some tasks, transfer learning using pre-trained models can significantly reduce training time and data requirements.

## Model Evaluation

After training, it's essential to evaluate your model's performance using test data. Keras provides the model.evaluate() method to compute various metrics like accuracy, loss, and more. You can also create custom evaluation metrics if needed.

## Overfitting and Underfitting

One common challenge in training deep learning models is overfitting, where the model performs well on the training data but poorly on unseen data. To combat overfitting, you can:

- Use dropout layers to randomly drop out neurons during training.

- Add regularization terms to the loss function.

- Increase the size of your training dataset.

- Simplify your model architecture.

Conversely, underfitting occurs when the model is too simple to capture the underlying patterns in the data. In such cases, you may need to increase the model's complexity or collect more data.

### Saving and Loading Models

Once you have a trained model, you can save it to disk using Keras' model.save() method. This allows you to later load the model and make predictions without retraining.

In practice, training deep learning models often involves a lot of experimentation and fine-tuning to achieve the desired performance. It's crucial to keep track of your experiments and document the best-performing models and hyperparameters.

In the next section, we'll explore transfer learning, a powerful technique that leverages pre-trained models for various tasks, saving both time and computational resources.

## Section 11.5: Transfer Learning and Model Deployment

Transfer learning is a technique in deep learning where a pre-trained neural network is used as the starting point for a new task. Instead of training a model from scratch, you leverage the knowledge captured by the pre-trained model, saving both time and computational resources. In this section, we'll explore transfer learning and discuss its applications.

### How Transfer Learning Works

Transfer learning works on the idea that the features learned by a neural network on one task can be useful for another related task. It's based on the assumption that lower-level features (e.g., edges, textures) learned by the initial layers of a deep network are generic and transferable.

The typical workflow of transfer learning involves these steps:

1. **Choose a Pre-trained Model**: Select a pre-trained model that was trained on a large, diverse dataset. Popular choices include models like VGG, ResNet, and Inception.
2. **Remove or Freeze Top Layers**: Remove the top layers (usually the classification layers) of the pre-trained model. These layers are task-specific and need to be replaced for your new task. Optionally, you can freeze the remaining layers to prevent them from being updated during training.
3. **Add Task-specific Layers**: Add new layers to the pre-trained model to adapt it to your specific task. These layers are typically a few fully connected layers followed by the output layer. The output layer's size depends on the number of classes in your new task.
4. **Train on Your Data**: Train the modified model on your task-specific dataset. Since you start with weights that already capture a lot of useful features, you usually require fewer training iterations and less data.

## Applications of Transfer Learning

Transfer learning has found success in various applications, including:

### *Image Classification*

For tasks like image classification, you can use pre-trained models like VGG, ResNet, or MobileNet to quickly build accurate classifiers for new categories of objects.

*Object Detection*

Transfer learning is valuable in object detection tasks, where you can fine-tune pre-trained models like Faster R-CNN or YOLO to detect custom objects in images or videos.

*Natural Language Processing (NLP)*

In NLP, you can use pre-trained models like BERT, GPT-3, or Word2Vec to improve the performance of tasks like sentiment analysis, text generation, and named entity recognition.

*Medical Imaging*

Transfer learning is used in medical imaging to leverage pre-trained models for tasks like disease diagnosis, tumor detection, and organ segmentation.

## Model Deployment

Once you have a trained model, deploying it for inference in real-world applications is a crucial step. Several options are available for model deployment:

- **Cloud Services**: Cloud providers like AWS, Google Cloud, and Azure offer cloud-based solutions for deploying machine learning models as APIs or serverless functions.
- **Edge Devices**: Deploying models on edge devices like smartphones, IoT devices, or edge servers allows for real-time inference without relying on cloud services.

TensorFlow Lite and ONNX Runtime are examples of frameworks for edge deployment.

• **Containerization**: Docker containers provide a portable way to package your model and its dependencies for deployment on various platforms.

• **Web Applications**: You can integrate your model into web applications using web frameworks like Flask or Django. This enables users to interact with your model through a web interface.

• **Mobile Apps**: If you're building mobile applications, frameworks like TensorFlow Lite for Android and Core ML for iOS make it easier to integrate machine learning models into your apps.

Remember that deploying a model involves considerations like scalability, security, and performance optimization. It's essential to choose the deployment method that best fits your application's requirements.

In conclusion, transfer learning is a valuable technique for leveraging pre-trained models and adapting them to new tasks, saving time and effort in model development. When deploying your models, consider the specific requirements of your application to choose the most suitable deployment strategy.

# Chapter 12: Natural Language Processing with NLTK and spaCy

## Section 12.1: Introduction to Natural Language Processing

Natural Language Processing (NLP) is a subfield of artificial intelligence (AI) that focuses on the interaction between computers and humans through natural language. It involves the development of algorithms and models that enable machines to understand, interpret, and generate human language. NLP has a wide range of applications, including chatbots, sentiment analysis, text summarization, language translation, and more.

### Key Challenges in NLP

NLP presents several challenges due to the complexity and ambiguity of human language. Some of the key challenges include:

1. **Ambiguity**: Words and phrases can have multiple meanings depending on the context. Resolving this ambiguity is a fundamental challenge in NLP.
2. **Syntax and Grammar**: Understanding the grammatical structure of sentences and documents is crucial for meaningful language processing.
3. **Named Entity Recognition (NER)**: Identifying and classifying entities such as names of people, organizations, locations, and dates in text.
4. **Coreference Resolution**: Determining when two or more words or phrases in a text refer to the same entity.
5. **Sentiment Analysis**: Analyzing and classifying the sentiment or emotional tone of a piece of text as positive,

negative, or neutral.

6. **Machine Translation**: Translating text from one language to another while preserving its meaning.
7. **Text Summarization**: Automatically generating concise summaries of longer texts.

## NLTK (Natural Language Toolkit)

NLTK is a Python library for working with human language data. It provides easy-to-use interfaces to over 50 corpora and lexical resources, such as WordNet. NLTK also includes a wide range of text processing libraries for tasks like tokenization, stemming, tagging, parsing, and semantic reasoning.

Let's take a brief look at NLTK's capabilities:

```
import nltk

# Download NLTK data (corpora and resources)

nltk.download()

# Tokenization

from nltk.tokenize import word_tokenize, sent_tokenize

text = "Natural Language Processing is fascinating. It has many applications."

words = word_tokenize(text)

sentences = sent_tokenize(text)

# Part-of-Speech Tagging

from nltk import pos_tag
```

```
tags = pos_tag(words)

# Named Entity Recognition (NER)

from nltk import ne_chunk

ner_tags = ne_chunk(tags)

# Stopwords Removal

from nltk.corpus import stopwords

stop_words = set(stopwords.words('english'))

# Stemming

from nltk.stem import PorterStemmer

stemmer = PorterStemmer()

stemmed_words = [stemmer.stem(word) for word in words]

# Lemmatization

from nltk.stem import WordNetLemmatizer

lemmatizer = WordNetLemmatizer()

lemmatized_words = [lemmatizer.lemmatize(word) for word in words]
```

NLTK is a powerful toolkit for NLP tasks and serves as an excellent starting point for working with text data in Python.

In the following sections of this chapter, we will explore more advanced NLP concepts and tools, including spaCy, a popular NLP library known for its speed and accuracy.

# Section 12.2: NLTK: Natural Language Toolkit

NLTK, which stands for Natural Language Toolkit, is a comprehensive Python library for natural language processing (NLP). It provides tools and resources for working with human language data, making it a valuable resource for tasks ranging from text analysis to machine learning. In this section, we will explore some of the key features and capabilities of NLTK.

## Installation

To get started with NLTK, you need to install it. You can use pip, the Python package manager, to install NLTK:

```
pip install nltk
```

## Basic Text Processing with NLTK

### *Tokenization*

Tokenization is the process of splitting text into individual words or tokens. NLTK provides various tokenization methods, including word tokenization and sentence tokenization.

```
import nltk

# Download NLTK data (if not already downloaded)

nltk.download()

# Tokenization

from nltk.tokenize import word_tokenize, sent_tokenize
```

```
text = "Natural Language Processing is fascinating. It has many applications."

words = word_tokenize(text)

sentences = sent_tokenize(text)

print(words)

print(sentences)
```

*Part-of-Speech Tagging*

NLTK allows you to perform part-of-speech tagging, which involves tagging each word in a sentence with its grammatical part of speech (e.g., noun, verb, adjective).

```
from nltk import pos_tag

tags = pos_tag(words)

print(tags)
```

*Named Entity Recognition (NER)*

Named Entity Recognition (NER) is the process of identifying and classifying named entities such as names of people, organizations, locations, and dates in text.

```
from nltk import ne_chunk

ner_tags = ne_chunk(tags)

print(ner_tags)
```

### *Stopwords Removal*

Stopwords are common words (e.g., "the," "and," "is") that are often removed from text data as they typically do not carry significant meaning.

```
from nltk.corpus import stopwords

stop_words = set(stopwords.words('english'))

filtered_words = [word for word in words if word.lower() not in stop_words]

print(filtered_words)
```

### *Stemming and Lemmatization*

NLTK provides tools for stemming and lemmatization, which are techniques for reducing words to their base or root forms.

```
from nltk.stem import PorterStemmer, WordNetLemmatizer

# Stemming

stemmer = PorterStemmer()

stemmed_words = [stemmer.stem(word) for word in words]

print(stemmed_words)

# Lemmatization

lemmatizer = WordNetLemmatizer()

lemmatized_words = [lemmatizer.lemmatize(word) for word in words]
```

```
print(lemmatized_words)
```

### Text Corpora and Resources

NLTK includes a wide range of text corpora and lexical resources that can be used for various NLP tasks. These resources cover different languages and domains, making them valuable for research and experimentation.

### Advanced NLP Tasks

While this section covers some fundamental NLP tasks with NLTK, the library offers much more, including syntactic parsing, machine learning for text classification, and sentiment analysis. Depending on your NLP project's requirements, NLTK provides the tools you need to work with text data effectively.

## Section 12.3: spaCy: Industrial-Strength NLP

spaCy is a popular and efficient Python library for natural language processing (NLP) tasks. It is designed to be fast, accurate, and easy to use, making it a valuable tool for both beginners and experienced NLP practitioners. In this section, we will explore some of the key features and capabilities of spaCy.

### Installation

You can install spaCy using pip:

```
pip install spacy
```

Once spaCy is installed, you will need to download a language model to work with. For example, to download the English language model, you can run:

```
python -m spacy download en_core_web_sm
```

## Basic Text Processing with spaCy

### *Tokenization*

Tokenization is the process of splitting text into individual words or tokens. spaCy provides built-in tokenization capabilities:

```
import spacy

# Load the English language model

nlp = spacy.load("en_core_web_sm")

# Tokenization

text = "Natural Language Processing is fascinating. It has many applications."

doc = nlp(text)

# Accessing tokens

tokens = [token.text for token in doc]

print(tokens)
```

### *Part-of-Speech Tagging*

spaCy allows you to perform part-of-speech tagging with ease:

```
# Part-of-speech tagging

pos_tags = [(token.text, token.pos_) for token in doc]

print(pos_tags)
```

### *Named Entity Recognition (NER)*

Named Entity Recognition (NER) is supported in spaCy, and you can identify named entities in text:

```
# Named Entity Recognition (NER)

ner_entities = [(ent.text, ent.label_) for ent in doc.ents]

print(ner_entities)
```

### *Dependency Parsing*

spaCy can perform dependency parsing, which involves determining the syntactic relationships between words in a sentence:

```
# Dependency parsing

dependency_tree = [(token.text, token.dep_) for token in doc]

print(dependency_tree)
```

## Advanced NLP Capabilities

spaCy offers more advanced NLP capabilities, including sentence segmentation, entity linking, text classification, and training custom models. The library is well-documented and has a strong user community, making it a versatile choice for various NLP projects.

## Efficiency and Production Use

One of spaCy's key advantages is its efficiency, making it suitable for production use. It is designed to process large volumes of text quickly, making it a top choice for applications that require real-time or batch NLP processing.

## Conclusion

spaCy is a powerful and efficient Python library for natural language processing tasks. It simplifies many NLP tasks while maintaining high accuracy, making it a valuable tool for text analysis, information extraction, and language understanding in various domains. Whether you are working on research projects or building production-ready NLP applications, spaCy is a library that can streamline your workflow and help you achieve your goals efficiently.

# Section 12.4: Text Classification and Sentiment Analysis

Text classification is a common natural language processing (NLP) task that involves categorizing text into predefined classes or labels. It has numerous applications, including sentiment analysis, spam detection, topic classification, and more. In this section, we will explore text classification and its practical implementation using Python libraries.

## Basics of Text Classification

Text classification is often performed using supervised machine learning techniques. The process typically involves the following steps:

1. **Data Collection:** Gather a labeled dataset where each text document is associated with a category or class label.
2. **Text Preprocessing:** Clean and preprocess the text data by removing noise, performing tokenization, and converting text to numerical features.
3. **Feature Extraction:** Extract relevant features from the text data, such as word frequencies, TF-IDF scores, or word embeddings.

4. **Model Training:** Train a machine learning model, such as a classifier (e.g., logistic regression, support vector machine, or deep learning models), using the labeled dataset and extracted features.
5. **Model Evaluation:** Assess the model's performance using evaluation metrics like accuracy, precision, recall, F1-score, and confusion matrices.
6. **Inference:** Use the trained model to classify new, unseen text documents into predefined categories.

## Sentiment Analysis

Sentiment analysis, a specific form of text classification, focuses on determining the sentiment or emotional tone expressed in a piece of text. It can be categorized into three main classes: positive, negative, or neutral sentiment. Sentiment analysis is widely used in social media monitoring, customer feedback analysis, and product reviews.

## Practical Implementation

Let's look at a practical example of sentiment analysis using Python's Natural Language Toolkit (NLTK) library. First, you need to install NLTK if you haven't already:

```
pip install nltk
```

Here's a simple code snippet to perform sentiment analysis using NLTK:

```
import nltk

from nltk.sentiment.vader import SentimentIntensityAnalyzer

# Download the VADER sentiment analysis lexicon (if not already downloaded)
```

```
nltk.download('vader_lexicon')

# Create a sentiment analyzer

sia = SentimentIntensityAnalyzer()

# Sample text

text = "I love this product! It's amazing."

# Perform sentiment analysis

sentiment_scores = sia.polarity_scores(text)

# Interpret the sentiment scores

if sentiment_scores['compound'] >= 0.05:

sentiment = "Positive"

elif sentiment_scores['compound'] <= -0.05:

sentiment = "Negative"

else:

sentiment = "Neutral"

print(f"Sentiment: {sentiment}")

print(f"Sentiment Scores: {sentiment_scores}")
```

In this example, we use the VADER (Valence Aware Dictionary and sEntiment Reasoner) sentiment analysis tool from NLTK. It provides a compound score that indicates the overall sentiment of the text.

## Conclusion

Text classification and sentiment analysis are essential NLP tasks with a wide range of practical applications. By leveraging Python libraries like NLTK, scikit-learn, or spaCy, you can implement text classification models to automatically analyze and categorize textual data, making it a valuable tool for various industries and domains.

# Section 12.5: Named Entity Recognition and Text Parsing

Named Entity Recognition (NER) is a subtask of Natural Language Processing (NLP) that focuses on identifying and classifying named entities within text. Named entities are specific pieces of information, such as names of people, organizations, locations, dates, and more. NER plays a crucial role in extracting structured information from unstructured text, making it valuable in various applications, including information retrieval, question answering, and text summarization.

## Basics of Named Entity Recognition

NER typically involves the following steps:

1. **Tokenization:** The input text is divided into individual words or tokens.
2. **Part-of-Speech Tagging:** Each token is tagged with its part of speech (e.g., noun, verb, adjective).
3. **Named Entity Recognition:** The tokens are classified into predefined categories or types, such as PERSON, ORGANIZATION, LOCATION, DATE, and others.
4. **Post-processing:** The recognized entities are often further processed, such as resolving co-references (e.g., "he" refers to "John Smith") and linking entities to external

knowledge bases (e.g., linking "New York City" to its Wikipedia page).

## Practical Implementation

Let's explore a practical example of Named Entity Recognition using the spaCy library in Python:

```
import spacy

# Load the spaCy model for English

nlp = spacy.load("en_core_web_sm")

# Sample text with named entities

text = "Apple Inc. is headquartered in Cupertino, California. John Smith, the CEO of the company, was born on January 15, 1975."

# Process the text with spaCy

doc = nlp(text)

# Extract named entities and their types

entities = [(ent.text, ent.label_) for ent in doc.ents]

# Print the recognized entities and their types

for entity, entity_type in entities:

print(f"Entity: {entity}, Type: {entity_type}")
```

In this code, we use spaCy's "en_core_web_sm" model, which is a small English language model pre-trained for NER. It identifies named entities and assigns them to categories like PERSON, ORGANIZATION, and DATE.

## Text Parsing

Text parsing involves analyzing the grammatical structure of a sentence to extract meaningful information. Parsing can be used to identify relationships between words, such as subject-verb-object relationships, and to break down complex sentences into their constituent parts. One common use case of text parsing is syntactic analysis to understand the grammatical structure of sentences.

Here's a simplified example of parsing using spaCy:

```
# Parse a sentence

sentence = "The quick brown fox jumps over the lazy dog."

parsed_sentence = nlp(sentence)

# Extract the grammatical structure

for token in parsed_sentence:

print(f"Token: {token.text}, Dependency: {token.dep_}, Head: {token.head.text}")
```

In this example, we use spaCy to parse a sentence and extract information about token dependencies and their heads, providing insights into the grammatical structure.

## Conclusion

Named Entity Recognition (NER) and text parsing are fundamental tasks in natural language processing that enable the extraction of structured information and the analysis of grammatical structures within text. Python libraries like spaCy, NLTK, and others provide powerful tools to perform NER and text parsing, making them accessible for a wide range of NLP applications.

# Chapter 13: Scientific Computing with SciPy

## Section 13.1: Overview of Scientific Computing

Scientific computing is a field of study that involves using computational techniques and tools to solve complex scientific and engineering problems. It plays a crucial role in various scientific disciplines, including physics, chemistry, biology, and engineering. Scientific computing often deals with mathematical modeling, data analysis, simulation, and numerical optimization.

### Why Scientific Computing?

Scientific computing is essential for several reasons:

1. **Complex Problem Solving:** Many scientific problems involve complex mathematical equations that cannot be solved analytically. Computational methods allow us to find numerical solutions.
2. **Data Analysis:** With the growing availability of data in various scientific domains, scientific computing tools are used for data analysis, visualization, and interpretation.
3. **Simulation:** Scientific simulations help researchers understand and predict the behavior of physical and biological systems. For example, simulating climate models or drug interactions.
4. **Optimization:** Optimizing parameters or designs is a common task in scientific research and engineering. Computational optimization techniques are crucial for finding optimal solutions.

5. **Parallel Processing:** Scientific computing often requires high-performance computing (HPC) and parallel processing to handle large datasets and simulations efficiently.

## The Role of SciPy

SciPy is an open-source library in Python that provides a wide range of mathematical and scientific computing tools. It builds on top of NumPy and provides additional functionality for optimization, integration, interpolation, eigenvalue problems, and more. SciPy is widely used in academia and industry for scientific research and engineering applications.

Let's explore some key components and capabilities of SciPy:

- **Integration:** SciPy provides functions for numerical integration, including single and multiple integration, quadrature, and more.

- **Optimization:** It offers optimization routines for finding minima (or maxima) of functions, constrained optimization, and nonlinear least-squares fitting.

- **Interpolation:** SciPy includes tools for interpolating data, such as splines, B-splines, and radial basis functions.

- **Linear Algebra:** The library contains functions for solving linear systems, eigenvalue problems, and matrix factorizations.

- **Statistics:** SciPy offers a wide range of statistical functions, including probability distributions, hypothesis testing, and statistical tests.

- **Signal and Image Processing:** It provides tools for signal processing, Fourier analysis, and image processing.

- **Sparse Matrices:** SciPy supports sparse matrix representations and efficient operations on large sparse matrices.

## Getting Started with SciPy

To use SciPy in your Python projects, you'll need to install it, along with NumPy, if you haven't already. You can install both libraries using pip:

```
pip install numpy scipy
```

Once installed, you can import and use SciPy modules in your Python scripts or notebooks. Here's an example of importing SciPy and using its optimization functions:

```
import numpy as np

from scipy.optimize import minimize

# Define an objective function to minimize

def objective(x):

return x[0]**2 + x[1]**2

# Initial guess

initial_guess = [1.0, 2.0]

# Minimize the objective function

result = minimize(objective, initial_guess)

print("Optimal solution:", result.x)
```

```
print("Optimal value:", result.fun)
```

In this example, we use SciPy's minimize function to find the minimum of a simple quadratic function.

## Conclusion

Scientific computing with SciPy empowers scientists, engineers, and researchers to tackle complex problems, perform data analysis, and conduct simulations. By providing a rich set of tools for mathematical modeling and analysis, SciPy has become an indispensable library in the scientific Python ecosystem. This chapter will delve deeper into the various capabilities of SciPy and how to leverage them for your scientific and engineering projects.

# Section 13.2: Numerical Methods with SciPy

In scientific computing, numerical methods are fundamental techniques for approximating solutions to mathematical problems. SciPy provides a comprehensive set of numerical methods that are widely used for solving a variety of scientific and engineering problems. In this section, we'll explore some of the key numerical methods available in SciPy.

## Root Finding

Finding the roots (or solutions) of equations is a common problem in scientific computing. SciPy provides several functions for root finding, including root, fsolve, and brentq. These functions are used to find the values of variables that make a given equation or system of equations equal to zero.

Here's an example of using the root function to find the roots of a simple equation:

```
from scipy.optimize import root

# Define the equation as a Python function

def equation(x):

return x**2 - 4

# Find the root of the equation

solution = root(equation, x0=2.0)

print("Root:", solution.x)
```

In this example, we define the equation as a Python function and use the root function to find its roots. The result is the value of x that satisfies the equation x^2 - 4 = 0.

## Numerical Integration

Numerical integration is used to approximate the definite integral of a function over a specified interval. SciPy provides the quad function for performing numerical integration. You can integrate both single and multiple functions using this function.

Here's an example of using the quad function to compute the integral of a simple function:

```
from scipy.integrate import quad

# Define the integrand as a Python function

def integrand(x):

return x**2

# Compute the definite integral of the function from 0 to 2
```

```
result, error = quad(integrand, 0, 2)

print("Integral:", result)

print("Error:", error)
```

In this example, we define the integrand as a Python function and use the quad function to compute the definite integral of the function x^2 from 0 to 2.

## Linear Algebra

SciPy provides a powerful set of functions for linear algebra operations, including solving linear systems of equations, eigenvalue problems, and matrix factorizations. These functions are part of the scipy.linalg module.

Here's an example of solving a linear system of equations using SciPy:

```
import numpy as np

from scipy.linalg import solve

# Define the coefficient matrix and right-hand side

A = np.array([[2, 1], [1, 3]])

b = np.array([3, 5])

# Solve the linear system Ax = b

x = solve(A, b)

print("Solution:", x)
```

In this example, we define the coefficient matrix A and the right-hand side b, and then use the solve function to find the solution x to the linear system Ax = b.

## Interpolation

Interpolation is the process of estimating values between known data points. SciPy provides functions for various interpolation methods, including linear, cubic, and spline interpolation. These functions are part of the scipy.interpolate module.

Here's an example of performing linear interpolation using SciPy:

```
from scipy.interpolate import interp1d

# Define some data points

x = [0, 1, 2, 3, 4]

y = [0, 1, 4, 9, 16]

# Create a linear interpolation function

interp_func = interp1d(x, y)

# Interpolate the value at x = 2.5

result = interp_func(2.5)

print("Interpolated value at x = 2.5:", result)
```

In this example, we define data points x and y, create a linear interpolation function using interp1d, and then interpolate the value at x = 2.5.

## Optimization

Optimization involves finding the minimum or maximum of a function. SciPy provides a wide range of optimization algorithms through the scipy.optimize module. You can perform unconstrained and constrained optimization using functions like minimize, fmin, and fmin_cobyla.

Here's an example of using the minimize function for unconstrained optimization:

```
from scipy.optimize import minimize

# Define an objective function to minimize

def objective(x):

return x[0]**2 + x[1]**2

# Initial guess

initial_guess = [1.0, 2.0]

# Minimize the objective function

result = minimize(objective, initial_guess)

print("Optimal solution:", result.x)

print("Optimal value:", result.fun)
```

In this example, we define an objective function and use the minimize function to find the minimum of the function starting from the initial guess.

## Conclusion

Numerical methods are essential tools in scientific computing,

# Section 13.3: Linear Algebra and Optimization

In this section, we will delve deeper into the capabilities of SciPy related to linear algebra and optimization. SciPy provides an extensive set of functions for solving linear algebra problems and performing optimization tasks, making it a powerful tool for scientific computing and data analysis.

## Linear Algebra with SciPy

### *Solving Linear Systems of Equations*

SciPy's scipy.linalg module offers functions to solve linear systems of equations. This can be incredibly useful in various applications such as solving engineering problems, simulating physical systems, or analyzing datasets.

Here's an example of using SciPy to solve a linear system:

```
import numpy as np

from scipy.linalg import solve

# Define the coefficient matrix A and the right-hand side b

A = np.array([[2, 1], [1, 3]])

b = np.array([3, 5])

# Solve the linear system Ax = b

x = solve(A, b)

print("Solution:", x)
```

In this example, we define the coefficient matrix A and the right-hand side vector b. The solve function computes the solution vector x such that Ax = b.

### *Eigenvalue Problems*

Eigenvalue problems are fundamental in many scientific fields, including physics, engineering, and computer graphics. SciPy provides functions like eig to compute the eigenvalues and eigenvectors of a matrix.

```
from scipy.linalg import eig

# Define a matrix

A = np.array([[4, 2], [1, 3]])

# Compute eigenvalues and eigenvectors

eigenvalues, eigenvectors = eig(A)

print("Eigenvalues:", eigenvalues)

print("Eigenvectors:\n", eigenvectors)
```

Here, we compute the eigenvalues and eigenvectors of matrix A.

## Optimization with SciPy

Optimization is a crucial task in scientific computing, machine learning, and many other domains. SciPy's scipy.optimize module provides a wide range of optimization algorithms for both constrained and unconstrained problems.

*Minimization Example*

Here's an example of using SciPy to minimize a mathematical function:

```
from scipy.optimize import minimize

# Define an objective function to minimize

def objective(x):

return x[0]**2 + x[1]**2

# Initial guess

initial_guess = [1.0, 2.0]

# Minimize the objective function

result = minimize(objective, initial_guess)

print("Optimal solution:", result.x)

print("Optimal value:", result.fun)
```

In this example, we define an objective function objective and use the minimize function to find the minimum value of this function starting from the initial guess.

## Conclusion

SciPy's capabilities in linear algebra and optimization make it a valuable library for scientific and engineering computations. Whether you need to solve linear systems of equations, compute eigenvalues, or perform optimization tasks, SciPy provides efficient and easy-to-use tools for these tasks. These functionalities are indispensable for tackling complex problems in various scientific and engineering disciplines.

## Section 13.4: Signal and Image Processing

In this section, we will explore the capabilities of SciPy related to signal and image processing. SciPy provides a rich set of functions and tools for working with signals and images, making it a valuable library for tasks like filtering, Fourier analysis, and image manipulation.

### Signal Processing with SciPy

#### *Filtering and Convolution*

SciPy offers functions for filtering and convolution, which are widely used in signal processing. You can perform operations like smoothing, sharpening, and noise reduction on signals using convolution.

Here's an example of smoothing a signal using SciPy:

```
import numpy as np

from scipy.signal import convolve

# Create a simple signal

signal = np.array([1, 2, 3, 4, 5])

# Define a smoothing kernel

kernel = np.array([1, 1, 1]) / 3

# Apply convolution to smooth the signal
```

```
smoothed_signal = convolve(signal, kernel, mode='valid')

print("Original Signal:", signal)

print("Smoothed Signal:", smoothed_signal)
```

In this example, we create a signal and define a smoothing kernel. The convolve function is then used to apply convolution and smooth the signal.

### *Fourier Analysis*

SciPy also provides tools for Fourier analysis, which is essential for understanding the frequency components of signals. You can perform tasks like Fourier transforms and spectral analysis.

```
import numpy as np

from scipy.fft import fft

# Create a sample signal

signal = np.sin(2 * np.pi * 5 * np.linspace(0, 1, 1000)) # 5 Hz sine wave

# Compute the FFT (Fast Fourier Transform)

spectrum = fft(signal)

print("Signal Spectrum:", spectrum)
```

In this example, we generate a 5 Hz sine wave and compute its FFT using SciPy's fft function. This allows us to analyze the frequency components of the signal.

## Image Processing with SciPy

### *Image Manipulation*

SciPy provides functions for basic image manipulation tasks, such as resizing, rotating, and cropping images. You can also perform pixel-level operations.

Here's an example of resizing an image using SciPy:

```
import numpy as np

from scipy import ndimage

import matplotlib.pyplot as plt

# Create a simple image (black square)

image = np.zeros((128, 128))

# Resize the image

resized_image = ndimage.zoom(image, 2)

# Display the original and resized images

plt.figure(figsize=(8, 4))

plt.subplot(121)

plt.imshow(image, cmap='gray')

plt.title("Original Image")

plt.subplot(122)

plt.imshow(resized_image, cmap='gray')
```

```
plt.title("Resized Image")

plt.show()
```

In this example, we create a simple black square image and then use SciPy's ndimage.zoom function to resize it.

### *Image Filtering*

You can apply various filters to images using SciPy. Filters like Gaussian, median, and Sobel filters are commonly used for tasks like blurring and edge detection.

```
import numpy as np

from scipy import ndimage

import matplotlib.pyplot as plt

# Create a simple image (white square on black background)

image = np.zeros((128, 128))

image[32:96, 32:96] = 1

# Apply a Gaussian filter to blur the image

blurred_image = ndimage.gaussian_filter(image, sigma=5)

# Display the original and blurred images

plt.figure(figsize=(8, 4))

plt.subplot(121)

plt.imshow(image, cmap='gray')

plt.title("Original Image")
```

```
plt.subplot(122)

plt.imshow(blurred_image, cmap='gray')

plt.title("Blurred Image")

plt.show()
```

In this example, we create an image with a white square on a black background and apply a Gaussian filter to blur it.

## Conclusion

SciPy's signal and image processing capabilities make it a versatile library for a wide range of tasks, including filtering, Fourier analysis, and image manipulation. Whether you're working with one-dimensional signals or two-dimensional images, SciPy provides efficient and easy-to-use tools for these operations. These functionalities are valuable for tasks like feature extraction, noise reduction, and image enhancement in fields like computer vision, image analysis, and signal processing.

# Section 13.5: Symbolic Mathematics with SymPy

In this section, we will explore the capabilities of SymPy, a Python library for symbolic mathematics. Unlike numerical computing libraries like NumPy and SciPy, SymPy is designed for symbolic computation, which means it can handle algebraic expressions, equations, calculus, and more in a symbolic form.

## Basic Symbolic Expressions

SymPy allows you to work with symbolic variables and create algebraic expressions. You can define symbols, perform basic arithmetic operations, and simplify expressions.

```
import sympy as sp

# Define symbolic variables

x, y = sp.symbols('x y')

# Create a symbolic expression

expression = x**2 + 2*x*y + y**2

# Simplify the expression

simplified_expression = sp.simplify(expression)

print("Original Expression:", expression)

print("Simplified Expression:", simplified_expression)
```

In this example, we define symbolic variables x and y, create a symbolic expression, and then simplify it using sp.simplify.

## Solving Equations

SymPy can also be used to solve equations symbolically. You can define equations and find solutions.

```
# Define an equation

equation = sp.Eq(x**2 - 4, 0)

# Solve the equation for x

solutions = sp.solve(equation, x)
```

```
print("Equation:", equation)

print("Solutions:", solutions)
```

Here, we define an equation x**2 - 4 = 0 and use sp.solve to find the solutions for x.

## Calculus

SymPy is a powerful tool for symbolic calculus. You can perform differentiation, integration, and limits symbolically.

```
# Differentiation

derivative = sp.diff(x**3 + 2*x**2 + x, x)

# Integration

integral = sp.integrate(3*x**2 + 4*x + 1, x)

# Limits

limit_result = sp.limit(1/x, x, 0)

print("Derivative:", derivative)

print("Integral:", integral)

print("Limit:", limit_result)
```

In this example, we calculate the derivative, integral, and limit of symbolic expressions.

## Linear Algebra

SymPy provides functionality for symbolic linear algebra, including matrix operations and solving linear systems.

```
# Define symbolic matrices and vectors

A = sp.Matrix([[1, 2], [3, 4]])

B = sp.Matrix([x, y])

C = sp.Matrix([5, 6])

# Matrix multiplication

product = A * B

# Solve a linear system

solution = sp.solve(A * B - C, [x, y])

print("Matrix Product:", product)

print("Linear System Solution:", solution)
```

Here, we define symbolic matrices A, B, and C, perform matrix multiplication, and solve a linear system.

## Conclusion

SymPy is a valuable library for symbolic mathematics in Python. It enables you to work with algebraic expressions, solve equations symbolically, perform calculus operations, and manipulate symbolic matrices. Whether you're working on symbolic algebra, calculus, or linear algebra problems, SymPy provides a convenient and powerful toolset for symbolic mathematics. This makes it useful in fields like mathematics, physics, engineering, and computer science where symbolic manipulation is essential for problem-solving and analysis.

# Chapter 14: Data Visualization with Bokeh and Plotly

## Section 14.1: Interactive Data Visualization

In this section, we will explore the world of interactive data visualization using two popular Python libraries, Bokeh and Plotly. Interactive data visualization allows you to create dynamic and engaging visual representations of your data that can be explored and manipulated by users.

### The Importance of Interactive Visualization

Static visualizations are great for conveying a snapshot of data, but they often fall short when it comes to exploring and understanding complex datasets. This is where interactive visualization shines. It allows users to interact with the data, zoom in, pan, filter, and get detailed information by hovering over elements. Interactive plots can be particularly valuable for data exploration, presentations, and dashboards.

### Introduction to Bokeh and Plotly

**Bokeh** is a powerful Python library for creating interactive and visually appealing web-based visualizations. It provides a high-level interface for creating a wide range of interactive plots, including scatter plots, line charts, bar charts, and more. Bokeh generates interactive HTML and JavaScript plots that can be embedded in web applications or notebooks.

**Plotly** is another versatile Python library for creating interactive visualizations. It supports a variety of chart types, from basic charts like scatter plots to complex ones like heatmaps and 3D plots.

Plotly's interactive plots can be used in web applications, dashboards, and Jupyter notebooks. It also offers an online platform for sharing and collaborating on data visualizations.

## Getting Started with Bokeh

To get started with Bokeh, you'll need to install it using pip:

```
pip install bokeh
```

Bokeh's main interface is the bokeh.plotting module, which provides a way to create plots and add interactive elements. Here's a simple example of creating a scatter plot with Bokeh:

```
from bokeh.plotting import figure, show

# Create a scatter plot

p = figure(title="Simple Scatter Plot", tools="pan,box_zoom,reset")

# Add data

x = [1, 2, 3, 4, 5]

y = [6, 7, 2, 4, 8]

p.circle(x, y, size=10, color="blue", alpha=0.5)

# Show the plot

show(p)
```

This code creates a scatter plot with Bokeh, adds some data points, and displays the plot using the show function. The resulting plot is interactive, allowing you to pan, zoom, and reset the view.

## Exploring Plotly

Plotly offers a Python library that allows you to create interactive plots with ease. To install Plotly, use the following command:

```
pip install plotly
```

Plotly provides a wide range of chart types and customization options. Here's an example of creating a basic scatter plot with Plotly:

```
import plotly.express as px

# Create a scatter plot

fig = px.scatter(x=[1, 2, 3, 4, 5], y=[6, 7, 2, 4, 8], title="Simple Scatter Plot")

# Show the plot

fig.show()
```

In this example, we use Plotly Express, a high-level interface for creating plots quickly. The scatter function is used to create a scatter plot, and fig.show() displays the interactive plot.

## Conclusion

Interactive data visualization is a powerful way to explore and communicate data. Bokeh and Plotly are two Python libraries that excel in creating interactive visualizations for a variety of applications. In the next sections, we will dive deeper into using Bokeh and Plotly to create more complex and interactive data visualizations.

## Section 14.2: Bokeh for Interactive Plots

In this section, we will explore Bokeh in more detail and learn how to create various types of interactive plots using this library. Bokeh is a versatile tool for interactive data visualization and can be used to create a wide range of plot types.

### Basic Scatter Plots

Let's start with a basic scatter plot using Bokeh. We will create a scatter plot to visualize the relationship between two variables, such as x and y coordinates. In this example, we'll use randomly generated data for demonstration purposes.

```
from bokeh.plotting import figure, show

import random

# Generate random data

x = [random.uniform(0, 1) for _ in range(100)]

y = [random.uniform(0, 1) for _ in range(100)]

# Create a Bokeh figure

p = figure(title="Basic Scatter Plot", tools="pan,box_zoom,reset")

# Add the scatter plot

p.circle(x, y, size=8, color="blue", alpha=0.7)

# Show the plot

show(p)
```

In this code snippet, we import Bokeh's figure and show functions. We generate random data for the x and y coordinates, create a scatter plot using the circle function, and finally, display the plot using show. The resulting plot is interactive, allowing you to pan, zoom, and reset the view.

## Line Charts

Bokeh can also be used to create line charts. Line charts are commonly used to visualize trends over time. Here's an example of creating a simple line chart:

```
from bokeh.plotting import figure, show

import random

# Generate random data

x = list(range(10))

y = [random.uniform(0, 1) for _ in range(10)]

# Create a Bokeh figure

p = figure(title="Simple Line Chart", tools="pan,box_zoom,reset")

# Add the line chart

p.line(x, y, line_width=2, color="green")

# Show the plot

show(p)
```

In this code, we generate random data for the x-axis (time) and y-axis (values). We create a line chart using the line function, specifying the line's width and color. Once again, the resulting plot is interactive.

## Bar Charts

Bokeh can also create bar charts. Bar charts are useful for comparing categories or displaying discrete data. Here's a basic example:

```
from bokeh.plotting import figure, show

# Data for the bar chart

categories = ["A", "B", "C", "D", "E"]

values = [5, 8, 3, 7, 2]

# Create a Bokeh figure

p = figure(x_range=categories, title="Simple Bar Chart", tools="pan,box_zoom,reset")

# Add the bar chart

p.vbar(x=categories, top=values, width=0.5, color="orange")

# Show the plot

show(p)
```

In this code, we specify the categories and corresponding values for the bar chart. We create a bar chart using the vbar function and specify the width and color of the bars. The resulting bar chart is interactive and can be customized further.

## Conclusion

Bokeh provides a wide range of tools for creating interactive plots, including scatter plots, line charts, bar charts, and more. This section has introduced you to the basics of creating these plots with Bokeh, and in the following sections, we will explore more advanced features and customization options offered by the library.

## Section 14.3: Advanced Bokeh Features

In this section, we will dive deeper into Bokeh and explore some of its advanced features and customization options. Bokeh offers a wide range of tools and options for creating interactive visualizations, and understanding these features can help you create more complex and tailored plots.

### Customizing Plot Appearance

Bokeh allows you to customize the appearance of your plots in various ways. You can control the colors, sizes, and styles of plot elements, such as markers and lines. Here's an example of customizing the appearance of a scatter plot:

```
from bokeh.plotting import figure, show

# Sample data

x = [1, 2, 3, 4, 5]

y = [5, 4, 3, 2, 1]

# Create a Bokeh figure

p = figure(title="Customizing Scatter Plot", tools="pan,box_zoom,reset")

# Customize the appearance of scatter points

p.circle(x, y, size=10, color="red", fill_alpha=0.6, line_color="black", line_width=2)
```

```
# Show the plot

show(p)
```

In this code, we use the circle method to create a scatter plot and customize the appearance of the scatter points. We set the size, color, fill alpha (transparency), line color, and line width to achieve the desired appearance.

## Annotations and Labels

Bokeh allows you to add annotations and labels to your plots to provide additional context and information. You can add text annotations, arrows, and labels easily. Here's an example of adding a text annotation to a plot:

```
from bokeh.plotting import figure, show

# Sample data

x = [1, 2, 3, 4, 5]

y = [5, 4, 3, 2, 1]

# Create a Bokeh figure

p = figure(title="Adding Text Annotation", tools="pan,box_zoom,reset")

# Add a text annotation

p.text(x=[3], y=[3], text=["Annotation"], text_font_size="14pt", text_color="navy")

# Show the plot

show(p)
```

In this code, we use the text method to add a text annotation to the plot at coordinates (3, 3). We can also specify the font size and text color.

## Hover Tools

One of Bokeh's powerful features is the ability to add hover tools to your plots. Hover tools display additional information when you hover over data points. Here's an example:

```
from bokeh.plotting import figure, show

from bokeh.models import HoverTool

# Sample data

x = [1, 2, 3, 4, 5]

y = [5, 4, 3, 2, 1]

names = ["A", "B", "C", "D", "E"]

# Create a Bokeh figure

p = figure(title="Adding Hover Tool", tools="pan,box_zoom,reset")

# Add a scatter plot

scatter = p.circle(x, y, size=10, color="green", legend_label="Points")

# Create a hover tool

hover = HoverTool()

hover.tooltips = [("Name", "@names"), ("Value", "@y")]

p.add_tools(hover)

# Show the plot
```

```
show(p)
```

In this code, we create a scatter plot and add a hover tool that displays the name and value of data points when hovering over them. We specify the tooltips using the tooltips property of the hover tool.

### Conclusion

Bokeh offers advanced features for customizing the appearance of plots, adding annotations and labels, and providing interactivity with tools like hover tools. These capabilities empower you to create sophisticated and interactive data visualizations for various applications. Experiment with these features to make your plots more informative and engaging.

## Section 14.4: Creating Dashboards with Plotly

In this section, we will explore how to create interactive dashboards using Plotly, a powerful Python library for data visualization. Dashboards are an excellent way to present complex data in a user-friendly and interactive manner, making it easier for users to explore and understand the data. Plotly provides tools for building web-based dashboards that can be shared and accessed through web browsers.

### Installing Plotly

Before we begin creating dashboards with Plotly, you need to ensure that you have Plotly installed. You can install Plotly using pip:

```
pip install plotly
```

## Basic Dashboard Components

A Plotly dashboard typically consists of one or more components such as graphs, charts, dropdowns, sliders, and buttons. These components are arranged in a layout to create an interactive interface.

Here's a simple example of a Plotly dashboard with a scatter plot and a dropdown:

```
import plotly.express as px

import dash

import dash_core_components as dcc

import dash_html_components as html

from dash.dependencies import Input, Output

# Sample data

df = px.data.iris()

# Initialize the Dash app

app = dash.Dash(__name__)

# Define the layout of the dashboard

app.layout = html.Div([

html.H1("Iris Data Dashboard"),

dcc.Dropdown(

id='dropdown',

options=[
```

```
{'label': 'Sepal Length', 'value': 'sepal_length'},
{'label': 'Sepal Width', 'value': 'sepal_width'},
{'label': 'Petal Length', 'value': 'petal_length'},
{'label': 'Petal Width', 'value': 'petal_width'}
],
value='sepal_length'
),
dcc.Graph(id='scatter-plot')
])
# Define callback to update the scatter plot based on dropdown selection
@app.callback(
Output('scatter-plot', 'figure'),
Input('dropdown', 'value')
)
def update_scatter_plot(selected_feature):
fig = px.scatter(df, x=selected_feature, y='species', title=f'Scatter Plot of {selected_feature} vs Species')
return fig
# Run the app
if __name__ == '__main__':
app.run_server(debug=True)
```

In this example, we use Plotly Express to create a scatter plot of iris dataset features. We also create a dropdown component that allows users to select a feature to display on the scatter plot. The dcc.Graph component displays the scatter plot, and we define a callback function to update the plot when the user selects a different feature from the dropdown.

## Conclusion

Plotly enables you to build interactive dashboards with a wide range of components and customization options. You can create dashboards to explore and visualize data, making it easier to derive insights and share them with others. Experiment with different components and layouts to create dashboards that best suit your data visualization needs.

# Section 14.5: Geographic and 3D Visualization

In this final section of Chapter 14, we'll delve into geographic and 3D visualization using Plotly, a versatile Python library for interactive data visualization. Plotly allows you to create visually appealing geographic maps and three-dimensional plots to visualize complex data relationships in an intuitive manner.

## Geographic Visualization

Plotly provides support for creating interactive geographic visualizations using geographical data. You can plot data on maps, customize markers, and create interactive features such as tooltips and zooming. Here's a basic example of plotting a map:

```
import plotly.express as px
```

```
# Sample data
df = px.data.gapminder().query("year==2007")
# Create a choropleth map
fig = px.choropleth(df,
locations="iso_alpha",
color="gdpPercap",
hover_name="country",
projection="natural earth",
title="World GDP per Capita (2007)")
# Show the map
fig.show()
```

In this example, we use the px.choropleth function to create a choropleth map of world GDP per capita in 2007. The locations parameter specifies the country codes, the color parameter defines the color scale based on GDP per capita, and hover_name provides the country names for tooltips. The projection parameter specifies the map projection.

## 3D Visualization

Plotly also supports 3D visualization, allowing you to create interactive 3D plots for visualizing complex data in three dimensions. Here's a simple 3D scatter plot example:

```
import plotly.express as px
# Sample data
```

```
df = px.data.iris()

# Create a 3D scatter plot

fig = px.scatter_3d(df, x="sepal_length", y="sepal_width", z="petal_length", color="species",

title="3D Scatter Plot of Iris Data")

# Show the 3D plot

fig.show()
```

In this example, we use the px.scatter_3d function to create a 3D scatter plot of iris dataset features. The x, y, and z parameters specify the variables for the three dimensions, and the color parameter assigns colors based on the species of iris flowers.

## Conclusion

Plotly offers powerful tools for geographic visualization and 3D plotting, allowing you to create interactive and visually appealing representations of your data. These techniques can be particularly useful when dealing with complex datasets that have geographic or multidimensional aspects. Experiment with Plotly's customization options to create compelling geographic maps and 3D visualizations tailored to your specific data analysis needs.

# Chapter 15: Geospatial Data Analysis with GeoPandas

## Section 15.1: Introduction to Geospatial Data

Geospatial data refers to data that is associated with specific geographic locations or features on the Earth's surface. This type of data often includes information about the geographical coordinates (latitude and longitude), boundaries of regions, and attributes related to these locations. Geospatial data is used in various fields, including geography, urban planning, environmental science, and more. Analyzing and visualizing geospatial data can provide valuable insights and support decision-making processes.

GeoPandas is a Python library that extends the capabilities of the popular data manipulation library, pandas, to handle geospatial data effectively. GeoPandas provides tools for reading, writing, analyzing, and visualizing geospatial data, making it a powerful tool for geospatial data analysis in Python.

### Key Concepts in Geospatial Data

Before diving into GeoPandas, it's essential to understand some fundamental concepts related to geospatial data:

1. **Geometry:** Geometry refers to the shapes and positions of geographic features. Geospatial data often involves different types of geometries, such as points, lines, and polygons, to represent objects like cities, roads, and land parcels.
2. **Geographic Coordinate System:** Geographic

coordinates, typically represented as latitude and longitude, are used to specify locations on the Earth's surface. Latitude measures north-south positions, while longitude measures east-west positions.

3. **Spatial Data Formats:** Geospatial data can be stored in various formats, including shapefiles, GeoJSON, and GeoTIFF. These formats define how geographic features and their attributes are structured and organized.
4. **Spatial Operations:** Spatial operations involve tasks like overlaying maps, calculating distances, and performing geometric transformations. These operations are crucial for geospatial analysis.
5. **Projections:** Earth's surface is three-dimensional, but maps are two-dimensional representations. Projections are methods for transforming the Earth's curved surface onto a flat map. Different projections have specific use cases and properties.

GeoPandas simplifies working with these concepts by providing a unified interface for geospatial data, allowing you to read, manipulate, and analyze geospatial datasets efficiently.

## Installing GeoPandas

To get started with GeoPandas, you can install it using pip:

pip install geopandas

Once installed, you can import GeoPandas in your Python scripts or notebooks to begin working with geospatial data.

In the upcoming sections, we'll explore GeoPandas in more detail, covering topics such as reading geospatial data, performing spatial operations, and creating geospatial visualizations.

## Section 15.2: Geopandas Basics

GeoPandas is a powerful Python library for working with geospatial data. It builds upon the capabilities of pandas, making it easier to handle and analyze geographic datasets. In this section, we will explore the core features and concepts of GeoPandas.

### Importing GeoPandas

To get started, you need to import GeoPandas. You can do this with the following import statement:

```
import geopandas as gpd
```

### GeoDataFrames and GeoSeries

GeoPandas introduces two fundamental data structures: GeoDataFrame and GeoSeries.

- **GeoDataFrame:** A GeoDataFrame is similar to a pandas DataFrame but with an additional geometry column that stores geometric information. This geometry column contains the spatial data, such as points, lines, or polygons.

- **GeoSeries:** A GeoSeries is similar to a pandas Series but specialized for spatial data. It consists of a series of geometric objects (e.g., points, lines) and their associated attributes.

### Reading Geospatial Data

GeoPandas provides functions to read various geospatial data formats, such as shapefiles, GeoJSON, and more. To read a shapefile, you can use the gpd.read_file() function:

```
gdf = gpd.read_file("path/to/shapefile.shp")
```

## Exploring Geospatial Data

Once you've loaded geospatial data into a GeoDataFrame, you can explore it just like you would with a regular pandas DataFrame. For example, you can use the head() method to view the first few rows of data:

```
print(gdf.head())
```

You can also access specific columns, perform filtering, and calculate statistics on your geospatial data.

## Geometry Operations

GeoPandas supports various geometry operations, allowing you to perform spatial operations on your data. For example:

- **Buffering:** You can create a buffer around geometric objects. This is useful for tasks like finding all points within a certain distance of a line.

```
buffered = gdf.buffer(distance=100) # Create a 100-unit buffer around each geometry
```

- **Intersection:** You can find the intersection of two GeoDataFrames. This is useful for tasks like finding overlapping polygons between two datasets.

```
intersection = gpd.overlay(gdf1, gdf2, how='intersection') # Find the intersection between gdf1 and gdf2
```

- **Spatial Joins:** You can perform spatial joins to combine data based on their spatial relationships.

result = gpd.sjoin(gdf1, gdf2, how="inner", op="intersects") # *Perform an intersect spatial join*

## Plotting Geospatial Data

GeoPandas makes it easy to visualize geospatial data. You can use the plot() method to create basic plots of your GeoDataFrame. For example:

gdf.plot()

GeoPandas leverages Matplotlib for plotting, so you can customize your plots further using Matplotlib functions.

These are the fundamental concepts of working with GeoPandas. In the next sections, we will explore more advanced topics, such as geospatial data manipulation, visualization, and analysis.

# Section 15.3: Geospatial Data Manipulation

In this section, we will delve deeper into geospatial data manipulation using GeoPandas. GeoPandas provides powerful tools for performing spatial operations, transforming data, and conducting various analyses on geographic datasets.

## Geometry Transformations

GeoPandas allows you to apply various transformations to geometries within a GeoDataFrame. Some common transformations include:

- **Scaling:** You can scale geometries by a factor in both the x and y dimensions.

  scaled_gdf = gdf.scale(xfact=2, yfact=2)

- **Translation:** You can translate (shift) geometries by specifying the x and y offsets.

translated_gdf = gdf.translate(xoff=10, yoff=10)

- **Rotation:** You can rotate geometries around a specified point.

rotated_gdf = gdf.rotate(angle=45, origin='center')

## Projections and Coordinate Reference Systems (CRS)

GeoPandas enables you to work with different Coordinate Reference Systems (CRS) and perform transformations between them. You can reproject a GeoDataFrame to a new CRS using the to_crs() method.

gdf = gdf.to_crs(epsg=3857) *# Reproject to Web Mercator (EPSG 3857)*

## Dissolving Geometries

Dissolving is a common operation where you merge features in a GeoDataFrame based on a shared attribute. This can be useful for aggregating data or simplifying boundaries. You can dissolve geometries based on a column value using the dissolve() method.

dissolved_gdf = gdf.dissolve(by='region', aggfunc='sum')

## Geometric Operations on GeoSeries

GeoPandas provides numerous geometric operations that can be applied to GeoSeries. Some examples include:

- **Area and Length:** You can calculate the area and length of geometries in a GeoSeries.

```
areas = gdf['geometry'].area

lengths = gdf['geometry'].length
```

- **Bounding Boxes:** You can create bounding boxes (envelopes) for geometries.

```
bounding_boxes = gdf['geometry'].envelope
```

- **Simplification:** You can simplify complex geometries.

```
simplified = gdf['geometry'].simplify(tolerance=10.0)
```

## Geocoding and Reverse Geocoding

GeoPandas can be integrated with geocoding services to convert between addresses and geographic coordinates (forward geocoding) or find addresses from coordinates (reverse geocoding). Although GeoPandas itself does not provide geocoding functionality, you can use external libraries or APIs in combination with GeoPandas to achieve this.

## Working with MultiGeometries

GeoPandas supports MultiGeometries, which are collections of multiple geometries in a single feature. MultiPoints, MultiLineStrings, and MultiPolygons are common examples. You can work with MultiGeometries just like single geometries.

```
multi_polygon = gdf['geometry'].unary_union # Merge multiple polygons into a single MultiPolygon
```

These are some of the advanced geospatial data manipulation techniques you can perform using GeoPandas. Depending on your specific analysis and visualization needs, GeoPandas provides a rich set of tools for working with geographic data efficiently and effectively.

## Section 15.4: Visualization and Mapping

Visualization is a crucial aspect of geospatial data analysis, and GeoPandas integrates seamlessly with popular Python libraries for creating maps and visualizing geographic data. In this section, we will explore techniques for visualizing and mapping geospatial data using GeoPandas.

### Basic Plotting

GeoPandas simplifies the process of creating basic maps by providing a convenient plot() method for GeoDataFrames and GeoSeries. When you call plot(), it generates a map with default settings, such as plotting polygons in different colors.

```
import geopandas as gpd

import matplotlib.pyplot as plt

# Create a GeoDataFrame (gdf) with geometries

gdf = gpd.read_file('shapefile.shp')

# Plot the GeoDataFrame

gdf.plot()

plt.show()
```

You can customize the appearance of the map by passing various arguments to the plot() method. For instance, you can specify the color, edge color, legend, and more.

## Customizing Maps

To create more customized maps, you can leverage the power of Matplotlib. After calling plot(), you can further modify the plot using Matplotlib functions. This allows you to add titles, labels, legends, and annotations.

```
# Create a GeoDataFrame (gdf) and plot it

gdf.plot()

# Customize the plot using Matplotlib

plt.title('Customized Map')

plt.xlabel('Longitude')

plt.ylabel('Latitude')

plt.legend(['Custom Legend'])

plt.show()
```

## Choropleth Maps

Choropleth maps are a common type of thematic map that color-codes areas based on a variable of interest. You can create choropleth maps using GeoPandas by specifying a column from your GeoDataFrame to determine the colors.

```
# Create a choropleth map based on a specific column

gdf.plot(column='population', legend=True)
```

```
plt.show()
```

## Overlaying Geometries

GeoPandas allows you to overlay multiple layers of geometries on a single map. This is useful for visualizing relationships or intersections between different datasets.

```
# Create two GeoDataFrames (gdf1 and gdf2) and plot them together

gdf1.plot()

gdf2.plot(ax=plt.gca(), color='red')

plt.show()
```

## Interactive Maps

For interactive maps, you can use libraries like Folium or Plotly in combination with GeoPandas. These libraries provide interactive features like zooming, panning, and pop-up information windows.

## Exporting Maps

Once you have created a map, you may want to save it as an image file (e.g., PNG, JPEG) or in a vector format (e.g., SVG). You can do this by using Matplotlib's savefig() function.

```
# Save the map as a PNG image

gdf.plot()

plt.savefig('map.png')
```

These are some of the techniques for visualizing and mapping geospatial data using GeoPandas. Depending on your project requirements, you can create a wide range of maps and visualizations to effectively communicate your insights from geographic datasets.

## Section 15.5: Spatial Analysis and Geocoding

Spatial analysis and geocoding are essential tasks in geospatial data analysis. Spatial analysis involves examining the relationships, patterns, and characteristics of geographic data, while geocoding is the process of converting addresses or place names into geographic coordinates (latitude and longitude). In this section, we will explore both spatial analysis techniques and geocoding using GeoPandas.

### Spatial Analysis

GeoPandas provides a variety of tools for performing spatial analysis on geospatial datasets. Some common spatial analysis tasks include:

*Buffering*

Buffering involves creating a zone around a set of features. This can be useful for analyzing proximity to certain locations. For example, you can create a buffer around a set of points to identify areas within a certain distance.

```
import geopandas as gpd

# Create a GeoDataFrame with points

gdf_points = gpd.read_file('points.shp')

# Create a buffer around the points (e.g., 1000 meters)

buffered = gdf_points.buffer(1000)
```

*Spatial Joins*

Spatial joins combine information from two GeoDataFrames based on their spatial relationship. You can perform operations like point-in-polygon joins, where you associate points with the polygons they fall within.

```
# Perform a point-in-polygon spatial join
join_result = gpd.sjoin(gdf_points, gdf_polygons, how='inner', op='intersects')
```

*Dissolving*

Dissolving combines adjacent polygons with the same attribute value into a single polygon. This is useful for aggregating data by a common attribute.

```
# Dissolve polygons based on a common attribute
dissolved = gdf_polygons.dissolve(by='category')
```

## Geocoding

Geocoding is the process of converting addresses or place names into geographic coordinates. GeoPandas can leverage external geocoding services or libraries for this task.

*Using Geopy*

The geopy library provides geocoding functionality. You can use it to obtain latitude and longitude coordinates for a given address.

```
from geopy.geocoders import Nominatim
```

```
geolocator = Nominatim(user_agent="geoapiExercises")

location = geolocator.geocode("New York City")

print((location.latitude, location.longitude))
```

## Spatial Analysis and Geocoding Libraries

While GeoPandas offers some spatial analysis capabilities, more advanced spatial analysis can be performed using libraries like Shapely for geometry operations, PySAL for spatial econometrics, and NetworkX for network analysis. These libraries complement GeoPandas and enable a broader range of spatial analysis tasks.

In this section, we've explored spatial analysis techniques such as buffering, spatial joins, and dissolving using GeoPandas. Additionally, we've briefly introduced geocoding with the geopy library. Depending on your geospatial analysis needs, you can employ these techniques to gain valuable insights from geographic datasets.

# Chapter 16: Testing and Debugging in Python

## Section 16.1: Importance of Testing and Debugging

Testing and debugging are integral parts of software development that help ensure the quality and reliability of your code. In this section, we'll delve into the significance of testing and debugging, exploring why they are crucial aspects of the development process.

### Why Testing Matters

Testing serves several vital purposes in software development:

1. **Identifying Bugs:** Testing helps identify and uncover bugs, errors, and unexpected behaviors in your code. By running tests, you can catch issues before they reach production.
2. **Ensuring Correctness:** Tests verify that your code functions correctly and produces the expected results. This is especially important in critical applications and systems.
3. **Regression Detection:** As your codebase evolves, changes and additions can inadvertently introduce new issues or break existing functionality. Testing helps detect regressions, ensuring that previously working features remain intact.
4. **Documentation:** Well-written tests serve as documentation for your code. They describe how your code is intended to work, making it easier for other developers to understand and contribute to the project.
5. **Refactoring Confidence:** Tests provide confidence when refactoring or making changes to your codebase. They act

as a safety net, allowing you to make improvements while knowing you won't introduce defects.

## The Debugging Process

Debugging is the process of identifying, isolating, and fixing issues in your code. It is a critical skill for developers, and here are some key aspects of debugging:

1. **Reproduction:** The first step in debugging is reproducing the issue. You need to determine the steps or conditions that lead to the problem.
2. **Isolation:** Once you can reproduce the problem, you need to isolate it. This involves pinpointing the specific code or component responsible for the issue.
3. **Diagnosis:** With the problem isolated, you can diagnose the root cause. This often involves inspecting variables, logs, and understanding the program's flow.
4. **Fixing:** After identifying the cause, you can implement a fix. It's crucial to test your fix to ensure it resolves the issue without introducing new problems.
5. **Prevention:** To prevent similar issues in the future, consider writing tests that cover the problem scenario. This way, you can catch regressions early.

## Types of Testing

There are various types of testing in software development, including:

- **Unit Testing:** Testing individual components or functions in isolation to ensure they behave as expected.

- **Integration Testing:** Verifying that different parts of your system work together correctly.

- **Functional Testing:** Testing the overall functionality of your application, often through automated end-to-end tests.

- **Regression Testing:** Re-running tests to ensure that new changes haven't introduced regressions.

- **Performance Testing:** Evaluating the speed and responsiveness of your software under different conditions.

### Testing Frameworks

Python offers numerous testing frameworks that make writing and running tests more efficient. Popular testing frameworks include unittest, pytest, and nose. These frameworks provide tools for organizing, running, and reporting on tests.

In the next sections of this chapter, we'll explore these testing frameworks, debugging techniques, and best practices for testing and debugging in Python. Testing and debugging are essential skills for any developer, and mastering them will contribute to the reliability and robustness of your software projects.

## Section 16.2: Writing Test Cases with unittest

unittest is a built-in testing framework in Python that provides a test discovery mechanism and various assertion methods for writing test cases. It is inspired by the JUnit testing framework and follows the xUnit style of testing. In this section, we will explore how to write test cases using unittest.

## Creating Test Cases

To create a test case using unittest, you need to define a class that inherits from unittest.TestCase. Each test case is a method within this class, and its name should start with the word "test." Here's an example of a simple test case:

```
import unittest

class MyTestCase(unittest.TestCase):

def test_addition(self):

result = 1 + 2

self.assertEqual(result, 3)

if __name__ == '__main__':

unittest.main()
```

In this example, we've defined a test case class MyTestCase with a single test method test_addition. Inside the test method, we perform an addition operation and use self.assertEqual to assert that the result is equal to 3.

## Running Tests

To run tests defined using unittest, you can execute the test file directly or use a test runner. If you execute the test file directly, make sure to include the following code at the end to run the tests:

```
if __name__ == '__main__':

unittest.main()
```

Alternatively, you can use the unittest test runner by running the following command in your terminal:

python -m unittest test_module

Replace test_module with the name of your test file without the ".py" extension. The test runner will discover and execute all test cases in the specified module.

## Assertion Methods

unittest provides a variety of assertion methods for verifying different conditions in your test cases. Some commonly used assertion methods include:

- assertEqual(a, b): Assert that a and b are equal.
- assertNotEqual(a, b): Assert that a and b are not equal.
- assertTrue(x): Assert that x is True.
- assertFalse(x): Assert that x is False.
- assertIn(item, container): Assert that item is in container.
- assertNotIn(item, container): Assert that item is not in container.

## Test Discovery

unittest supports test discovery, which means it can automatically find and run all test cases in a project. To enable test discovery, you should organize your test files and test case classes following a specific naming convention.

- Test files should be named with the prefix test_, e.g., test_math.py.

- Test case classes should be named with the prefix Test, e.g., TestMathOperations.

By adhering to these naming conventions, you can run test discovery using the unittest test runner without specifying individual test files or classes. This is particularly useful for larger projects with many test cases.

In the next sections, we will explore more advanced features of unittest, such as test fixtures, test suites, and test runners. Writing comprehensive and organized test cases using unittest is essential for maintaining the quality and reliability of your Python code.

# Section 16.3: Debugging Techniques and Tools

Debugging is a crucial skill for developers to identify and resolve issues in their code. Python provides various debugging techniques and tools to help you track down and fix problems in your programs. In this section, we'll explore some essential debugging techniques and tools that can make your debugging process more efficient.

## 1. Printing Debugging Statements

The most straightforward debugging technique is to insert print statements in your code to display variable values, control flow, and other information. You can use the print() function to print messages and variables to the console. For example:

```
def calculate_sum(a, b):

print(f"Calculating sum of {a} and {b}")
```

```
result = a + b
print(f"Result: {result}")
return result
```

By strategically placing print() statements, you can trace the execution flow and inspect variable values at different points in your code.

## 2. Using pdb - The Python Debugger

Python has a built-in interactive debugger called pdb, which allows you to set breakpoints, step through code, and inspect variables interactively. To use pdb, you can insert the following line where you want to start debugging:

```
import pdb; pdb.set_trace()
```

When your program reaches this line, it will pause execution, and you'll be dropped into an interactive debugger session. From there, you can use various pdb commands like n (next), c (continue), p (print), and q (quit) to navigate and debug your code.

## 3. Using Integrated Development Environments (IDEs)

Many integrated development environments (IDEs) for Python come with built-in debugging tools that provide a more user-friendly debugging experience than pdb. Popular Python IDEs like PyCharm, Visual Studio Code, and PyDev offer features like setting breakpoints, variable inspection, and step-by-step debugging.

To use these features, you typically set breakpoints by clicking on the left margin of your code editor, run your code in debug mode, and then step through your code while observing variable values and the call stack.

## 4. Logging

The logging module in Python is a powerful tool for debugging and monitoring applications. You can use it to log messages with different severity levels (e.g., debug, info, warning, error) to various destinations (e.g., console, file).

Here's an example of how to set up a basic logger:

```
import logging

logging.basicConfig(level=logging.DEBUG)

logger = logging.getLogger(__name__)

def calculate_sum(a, b):

logger.debug(f"Calculating sum of {a} and {b}")

result = a + b

logger.debug(f"Result: {result}")

return result
```

By configuring logging, you can control the verbosity of your application's debug output and save logs for future reference.

## 5. Third-Party Debuggers

In addition to built-in and IDE-specific debugging tools, you can also use third-party debuggers like pdb++ and ipdb, which enhance the debugging experience with additional features and capabilities.

These debuggers provide syntax highlighting, improved navigation, and better introspection.

To use ipdb, you can install it via pip and use it like pdb:

```
import ipdb; ipdb.set_trace()
```

Debugging is an essential skill for every programmer, and Python offers a variety of tools and techniques to make the process more effective. By mastering these debugging techniques, you can troubleshoot and fix issues in your code more efficiently, resulting in more reliable and robust applications.

## Section 16.4: Test Automation with pytest

Automated testing is an integral part of software development, ensuring that your code functions correctly and remains stable as it evolves. In Python, pytest is a popular testing framework that simplifies the process of writing and running tests. In this section, we'll explore how to use pytest to automate the testing of your Python code.

### Installing pytest

Before using pytest, you need to install it. You can do this via pip, the Python package manager, as follows:

```
pip install pytest
```

### Writing Test Functions

pytest uses a straightforward naming convention to discover and run test functions. To create a test, you simply create a Python function whose name starts with "test_". For example:

```
# test_math_operations.py

def test_addition():

assert 1 + 1 == 2

def test_subtraction():

assert 3 - 1 == 2

def test_multiplication():

assert 2 * 3 == 6

def test_division():

assert 6 / 2 == 3
```

In this example, we have defined four test functions, each testing a different mathematical operation. The assert statements check whether the expressions are true, and if not, pytest reports a failure.

## Running Tests

To run your tests, open a terminal, navigate to the directory containing your test files, and execute the following command:

```
pytest
```

pytest will automatically discover and run all the test functions in the files that match the naming convention. You will see output indicating which tests passed and which failed.

## Test Discovery

pytest uses powerful test discovery mechanisms to find and run your tests. By default, it discovers test files named test_*.py or *_test.py and test functions with names starting with "test_". You can customize this behavior using various command-line options or by configuring a pytest.ini file.

## Parametrized Tests

pytest allows you to write parametrized tests, which run the same test logic with different input values. This is useful for testing multiple cases with minimal code duplication. Here's an example:

```
# test_parametrized.py

import pytest

@pytest.mark.parametrize("input, expected", [(1, 2), (3, 6), (5, 10)])

def test_double(input, expected):

result = input * 2

assert result == expected
```

In this test, we use the @pytest.mark.parametrize decorator to specify a list of input and expected output pairs. pytest will run the test function multiple times, once for each pair, and report the results individually.

## Fixtures

Fixtures are a powerful feature in pytest that allow you to set up and tear down resources required for testing. For example, you can use fixtures to create a clean database connection or set up a temporary directory for file operations. Fixtures are defined as functions with the @pytest.fixture decorator and can be injected into test functions as arguments.

Here's an example of a fixture for creating a temporary directory:

```
# conftest.py

import pytest

import tempfile

import shutil

@pytest.fixture(scope="function")

def temp_directory(request):

temp_dir = tempfile.mkdtemp()

yield temp_dir

shutil.rmtree(temp_dir)
```

In this fixture, we create a temporary directory, yield it, and then remove it after the test function has finished.

## Conclusion

pytest is a versatile and easy-to-use testing framework for automating the testing of your Python code. With its straightforward naming conventions, powerful test discovery mechanisms, parametrized tests, and fixtures, pytest simplifies the process of writing and running tests, helping you maintain code quality and catch regressions as your projects evolve. Incorporating automated testing into your development workflow is a best practice that can save you time and prevent bugs in the long run.

# Section 16.5: Continuous Integration and Testing

Continuous Integration (CI) is a software development practice that involves automatically building, testing, and deploying your code changes to a shared repository. This approach helps identify and resolve integration issues early in the development process, ensuring that your code is always in a deployable state. In this section, we'll explore the concepts of CI and how to integrate automated testing into your CI workflow.

## Why Use Continuous Integration?

The main benefits of CI include:

1. **Early Issue Detection:** CI systems automatically build and test your code changes as soon as they are pushed to the repository. This early feedback helps identify issues and bugs before they impact your production environment.
2. **Consistency:** CI ensures that code is built and tested consistently across different environments and platforms, reducing the "it works on my machine" problem.
3. **Efficiency:** CI automates repetitive tasks like building, testing, and deploying code changes, saving developers time and allowing them to focus on writing code.
4. **Collaboration:** CI encourages collaboration by providing a central location for all team members to see the status of the codebase. It also helps avoid conflicts by detecting merge issues early.

## Setting Up Continuous Integration

To set up CI for your Python project, you'll need the following components:

1. **Version Control System (VCS):** Use a VCS like Git to manage your codebase. Popular platforms like GitHub, GitLab, and Bitbucket support Git and provide CI integration.
2. **CI Service:** Choose a CI service that integrates with your VCS. Some popular options for Python projects are Travis CI, CircleCI, GitHub Actions, and GitLab CI/CD.
3. **Configuration File:** Create a configuration file (e.g., .travis.yml for Travis CI) in your project's root directory. This file defines the CI workflow, including build and test instructions.

Here's an example .travis.yml file for a Python project using Travis CI:

```
language: python

python:

- 3.8

- 3.9

install:

- pip install -r requirements.txt

script:

- pytest
```

In this example, we specify the Python versions to test, install project dependencies, and run tests using pytest.

## CI Workflow

The typical CI workflow for a Python project includes the following steps:

1. **Push Code Changes:** Developers push code changes to the VCS, triggering the CI process.
2. **Build:** The CI service clones the repository and sets up a clean environment. It then installs dependencies, compiles code (if necessary), and prepares the project for testing.
3. **Test:** Automated tests, including unit tests and integration tests, are executed. If any tests fail, the CI pipeline reports a failure.
4. **Artifact Generation:** After successful tests, the CI system can generate artifacts, such as deployable packages or documentation.
5. **Deployment (Optional):** For some projects, CI includes deployment steps to staging or production environments.
6. **Notification:** The CI service notifies the team of the build and test results, including success or failure.

## Continuous Deployment (CD)

Continuous Deployment extends the CI concept to automatically deploy code changes to production if all tests pass. While CI focuses on ensuring that code is always in a deployable state, CD takes it a step further by automating the deployment process.

When implementing CD, it's crucial to have proper safeguards in place, like automated tests, quality gates, and manual approvals, to prevent potentially harmful code changes from being deployed directly to production.

## Conclusion

Continuous Integration and Testing are essential practices in modern software development. By setting up a CI/CD pipeline for your Python projects, you can catch issues early, ensure code quality, and streamline the development process. Incorporating CI/CD into your workflow helps you deliver reliable and high-quality software to your users while maintaining a smooth and collaborative development environment.

# Chapter 17: Packaging and Distribution

## Section 17.1: Packaging Python Projects

Packaging is a crucial aspect of Python development, as it allows you to distribute your code, libraries, or applications to other developers or users. Properly packaging your Python projects ensures that they can be easily installed and used by others. In this section, we'll explore the fundamentals of packaging Python projects.

## Why Package Python Projects?

Packaging serves several purposes:

1. **Distribution:** Packaging makes it easy to distribute your Python code, allowing other developers to use your libraries or applications without needing to understand the internal details.
2. **Dependency Management:** Packages specify their dependencies, ensuring that the required libraries or modules are installed automatically when someone installs your package.
3. **Versioning:** You can assign version numbers to your packages, making it clear which version of your code is

being used and allowing users to specify the version they want to install.

4. **Isolation:** Packaging provides isolation by creating separate environments for different projects, preventing conflicts between dependencies.

## The Anatomy of a Python Package

A Python package typically consists of the following elements:

1. **Module Files:** These are the .py files that contain the actual code. Modules can be organized into subdirectories.
2. **__init__.py:** This special file makes a directory a Python package. It can be empty or contain initialization code for the package.
3. **setup.py:** This script contains metadata about the package, including its name, version, author, and dependencies. It's used for building and distributing the package.
4. **README.md:** A documentation file that provides information about the package, how to install it, and how to use it.
5. **requirements.txt:** A file that lists the dependencies required for the package to work. It's commonly used with tools like pip for dependency management.

## Creating a Python Package

To create a Python package, follow these steps:

1. **Organize Your Code:** Place your Python modules (.py files) in a directory. You can also create subdirectories to organize your code logically.
2. **Add __init__.py:** If it doesn't exist already, create an __init__.py file in the package's root directory. This file can

be empty or contain package-level initialization code.

3. **Write setup.py:** Create a setup.py script in the package's root directory. This script uses the setuptools library to define package metadata and dependencies. Here's a minimal example:

```
from setuptools import setup, find_packages

setup(

name="mypackage",

version="0.1",

packages=find_packages(),

install_requires=[

# List your dependencies here

],

)
```

1. **Write Documentation:** Create a README.md file in the package's root directory to provide documentation for your package.
2. **Specify Dependencies:** If your package has dependencies, list them in a requirements.txt file.

## Building and Distributing a Package

Once you've created your Python package, you can build and distribute it using setuptools. Here are the basic steps:

1. **Build:** Use the setuptools sdist command to create a source

distribution of your package:

```
python setup.py sdist
```

1. **Distribution:** The source distribution will be created in the dist directory. You can share this distribution with others.
2. **Installation:** To install your package locally, you can use pip:

```
pip install .
```

1. **Upload to PyPI (Optional):** If you want to make your package available to the wider Python community, you can upload it to the Python Package Index (PyPI) using twine:

```
pip install twine

twine upload dist/*
```

## Conclusion

Packaging is a fundamental skill for Python developers, enabling you to share your code and libraries with others. By properly packaging your Python projects, you make it easier for users to install and use your software, manage dependencies, and keep track of versions. Understanding the basics of packaging is essential for anyone looking to contribute to the Python ecosystem or distribute their own Python packages.

# Section 17.2: Creating Python Packages

Creating Python packages is a fundamental skill for developers who want to share their code and libraries with others. In the previous section, we discussed the basics of packaging Python projects. Now, we'll dive deeper into the process of creating Python packages step by step.

## Step 1: Organize Your Code

Before you can create a Python package, you need to organize your code into a directory structure. This structure typically includes your Python module files (.py) and can also have subdirectories for better organization. For example, you might structure your code like this:

mypackage/

mymodule.py

mysubpackage/

__init__.py

submodule1.py

submodule2.py

In this example, mypackage is the root package, mymodule.py is a module within the package, and mysubpackage is a subpackage containing its own modules.

## Step 2: Add __init__.py

In Python, a directory is considered a package when it contains an __init__.py file. This file can be empty or can contain package-level initialization code. Its presence signals to Python that the directory should be treated as a package.

## Step 3: Write setup.py

To make your code installable as a package, you need to create a setup.py script. This script uses the setuptools library to define package metadata and dependencies. Here's a simplified example of a setup.py script:

```
from setuptools import setup, find_packages

setup(

name="mypackage",

version="0.1",

packages=find_packages(),

install_requires=[

# List your dependencies here

],

)
```

In this script, replace "mypackage" with your package's name, "0.1" with the desired version, and provide a list of dependencies in the install_requires field.

## Step 4: Write Documentation

A good package includes documentation to help users understand how to use it. Create a README.md file in the package's root directory and fill it with information about your package, installation instructions, usage examples, and any other relevant details.

## Step 5: Specify Dependencies

If your package has external dependencies (other Python packages it relies on), you can specify them in a requirements.txt file. This file lists the required packages and their versions, making it easier for users to set up their environment. Here's an example requirements.txt:

```
numpy>=1.20

pandas>=1.3
```

## Step 6: Build the Package

To create a source distribution of your package, run the following command in the package's root directory:

```
python setup.py sdist
```

This command will create a .tar.gz file in the dist directory, which is the source distribution of your package.

## Step 7: Install Locally

You can install your package locally for testing and development purposes. Use pip to install the package from the current directory:

```
pip install .
```

This command tells pip to install the package using the setup.py script in the current directory.

## Step 8: Distribution (Optional)

If you want to share your package with others, you can upload it to the Python Package Index (PyPI) or another distribution platform.

To upload to PyPI, you'll need to use a tool like twine. First, install twine:

```
pip install twine
```

Then, upload your package:

```
twine upload dist/*
```

## Conclusion

Creating Python packages involves organizing your code, adding necessary files like __init__.py and setup.py, documenting your package, specifying dependencies, and building the package for distribution. Properly packaging your code makes it easier for others to install and use, and it encourages collaboration and code sharing within the Python community. Understanding the package creation process is essential for Python developers who want to contribute to open-source projects or distribute their own libraries and applications.

# Section 17.3: Distribution and Publishing

Once you've created a Python package, the next step is distribution and publishing. Distributing your package allows others to easily install and use it. In this section, we'll explore the various methods and platforms for distributing and publishing Python packages.

## PyPI (Python Package Index)

The Python Package Index, commonly known as PyPI, is the primary platform for distributing Python packages. It hosts thousands of Python libraries and packages, making it the go-to repository for Python developers. To publish your package on PyPI, follow these steps:

1. **Create a PyPI Account:** You need to create an account on PyPI if you don't already have one.
2. **Prepare Your Package:** Ensure your package has a setup.py file with the necessary metadata, as discussed in the previous section (Section 17.2).
3. **Build Your Package:** Build a source distribution of your package using the python setup.py sdist command. This will create a .tar.gz file in the dist directory.
4. **Upload Your Package:** Use twine, a package for uploading distributions to PyPI, to upload your package. Install twine with pip install twine if you haven't already. Then, run twine upload dist/* to upload your package.
5. **Release Your Package:** After uploading, you can release your package on PyPI, making it available to others. You can do this manually through the PyPI website or use tools like twine to automate the process.
6. **Install Your Package:** Users can install your package using pip install your-package-name.

## Conda (Anaconda/Miniconda)

If your package includes binary dependencies or you want to target a wider audience, you can distribute it through Conda. Conda is a cross-platform package manager that works with Python and other languages. Here's how to distribute your package using Conda:

1. **Create a Conda Recipe:** Conda packages are defined by "recipes." Create a meta.yaml file with the package's metadata and dependencies.
2. **Build Conda Packages:** Use conda build to create Conda packages from your recipe. This generates platform-specific packages (e.g., for Linux, macOS, and Windows).
3. **Upload to Conda Repository:** You can host your Conda

packages on Anaconda Cloud or a custom Conda repository. Upload your packages using conda upload.

4. **Install with Conda:** Users can install your Conda package using conda install your-package-name.

## GitHub

If you want to distribute your package directly from a version control repository (e.g., GitHub), you can do so using pip:

1. **Create a GitHub Repository:** Host your package's source code on GitHub.
2. **Release on GitHub:** Create releases on GitHub with version tags. Include source distribution files (e.g., .tar.gz) as release assets.
3. **Install with pip:** Users can install your package directly from GitHub using pip install git+https://github.com/username/repo.git@tag-or-branch.

## Custom Repositories

You can also set up custom repositories to distribute packages privately or to a specific audience. Tools like devpi and pulp allow you to manage your package repository, control access, and distribute packages within your organization.

## Docker

For distributing packages in containerized environments, consider creating Docker images containing your package and its dependencies. Docker Hub and other container registries allow you to host and share these images.

### Package Managers

Package managers like conda, pipenv, and poetry provide ways to manage dependencies and package distribution. They can simplify the installation process for users.

### Continuous Integration (CI)

Integrate your package distribution process with a CI/CD (Continuous Integration/Continuous Deployment) system. This ensures that new versions of your package are automatically built, tested, and published when changes are pushed to your version control repository.

### Documentation and Support

Don't forget to maintain documentation for your package, including installation instructions, usage examples, and API documentation. Provide support channels for users to ask questions or report issues, such as GitHub issues or a dedicated mailing list.

By distributing your Python package effectively, you enable others to benefit from your work and contribute to the broader Python ecosystem. Choosing the right distribution methods and platforms depends on your package's goals and target audience.

## Section 17.4: Managing Dependencies with Pip

Managing dependencies is a crucial aspect of Python package development and distribution. Properly specifying and managing dependencies ensures that your package can be installed and run correctly on various systems. In this section, we will focus on using pip to manage dependencies for your Python packages.

## Understanding Dependencies

Dependencies are external Python packages or modules that your package relies on to function correctly. These dependencies can be categorized into two main types:

1. **Runtime Dependencies:** These are packages that your package needs to run successfully. For example, if your package uses the NumPy library, NumPy is a runtime dependency.
2. **Development Dependencies:** These are packages that are only needed during the development and testing phase of your package. For example, testing frameworks like pytest are development dependencies.

## Specifying Dependencies

You need to specify your package's dependencies in a format that pip can understand. This is typically done in a requirements.txt file or within your package's setup.py file. Here's how to do it:

### *Using requirements.txt*

Create a file named requirements.txt in your package's root directory and list the dependencies one per line. For example:

numpy>=1.19.0

pandas>=1.3.0

In this example, we specify that our package requires NumPy version 1.19.0 or higher and pandas version 1.3.0 or higher.

*Using setup.py*

You can also specify dependencies directly in your setup.py file using the install_requires parameter. For example:

```
from setuptools import setup

setup(

name="your-package",

version="1.0.0",

install_requires=[

"numpy>=1.19.0",

"pandas>=1.3.0",

],

# Other package metadata...

)
```

## Installing Dependencies

To install the dependencies for your package, users can use the following pip command:

```
pip install -r requirements.txt
```

If dependencies are specified within the setup.py file, pip will automatically resolve and install them when users install your package:

```
pip install your-package
```

### Dependency Management Best Practices

Here are some best practices for managing dependencies effectively:

1. **Be Specific:** Specify precise version ranges for your dependencies to avoid unexpected issues due to breaking changes in newer versions.
2. **Use Virtual Environments:** Encourage users to use virtual environments for their projects to isolate package installations.
3. **Update Regularly:** Keep your package's dependencies up to date to benefit from bug fixes and new features.
4. **Check Compatibility:** Test your package with different versions of its dependencies to ensure compatibility.
5. **Document Dependencies:** Include a clear list of dependencies in your package's documentation, including their purpose and any special considerations.
6. **Security:** Regularly check for security vulnerabilities in your package's dependencies and update them accordingly.
7. **Consider Alternative Implementations:** Some packages may have alternative implementations or forks that better suit your needs or have fewer dependencies.

By following these best practices, you can ensure that your package's dependencies are managed effectively, making it easier for users to install and use your package without encountering compatibility or version conflicts.

## Section 17.5: Best Practices for Packaging

Packaging Python projects is a crucial step in making them easily distributable and accessible to other developers. Well-packaged projects are more likely to be used, maintained, and integrated into other applications. In this section, we will discuss some best practices for packaging Python projects.

## 1. Use a Standard Structure

Follow a standard project structure to organize your code and assets. A common structure includes directories for source code, tests, documentation, and other project-related files. Tools like cookiecutter can help you create project templates with the recommended structure.

```
my_package/

my_package/

__init__.py

module1.py

module2.py

tests/

test_module1.py

test_module2.py

README.md

LICENSE

setup.py
```

## 2. Include a README

Write a clear and informative README file that explains what your project does, how to install it, and how to use it. A well-documented project is more likely to be adopted by others. Use Markdown or reStructuredText for your README for better formatting.

### 3. Use Version Control

Use a version control system like Git to track changes to your project. Hosting your code on platforms like GitHub or GitLab makes it easy for others to collaborate, report issues, and contribute.

### 4. Include a License

Choose an open-source license for your project to specify how others can use, modify, and distribute it. Common licenses include MIT, BSD, and Apache. Including a license is essential for legal clarity and encourages contributions.

### 5. Package Metadata

Provide metadata about your project in the setup.py file, including the project's name, version, author, and description. This information is used when publishing your package on the Python Package Index (PyPI) or other package repositories.

```
from setuptools import setup, find_packages

setup(

name="my_package",

version="0.1.0",

author="Your Name",

description="A short description of your project",

packages=find_packages(),
```

```
install_requires=[
# List your dependencies here
],
)
```

## 6. Testing

Write unit tests for your code to ensure its correctness and reliability. Tools like unittest or pytest can help you write and run tests effectively. Continuous integration services like Travis CI or GitHub Actions can automatically run tests on each code push.

## 7. Document Your Code

Use docstrings and documentation tools like Sphinx to generate clear and accessible documentation for your project. Well-documented code is easier to maintain and contributes to a better developer experience.

## 8. Continuous Integration

Set up continuous integration (CI) pipelines to automatically build, test, and deploy your project. CI ensures that your code remains functional and compatible with different Python versions and dependencies.

## 9. Release Workflow

Define a release workflow for your project. Semver (Semantic Versioning) is a common versioning scheme that helps users understand the compatibility and impact of version changes.

## 10. Publish to PyPI

If you want your package to be widely accessible, consider publishing it on PyPI. Use twine to create and upload distributions. Ensure that your package name is unique to avoid conflicts.

By following these best practices, you can create well-structured, maintainable, and accessible Python packages that are more likely to gain adoption within the Python community.

# Chapter 18: Performance Optimization

Performance optimization is a critical aspect of software development, especially in Python, where execution speed can sometimes be a concern. In this chapter, we will explore various techniques and strategies to optimize the performance of Python code. We'll cover profiling, memory optimization, Just-In-Time (JIT) compilation with Cython, parallel and concurrent programming, and performance tuning strategies.

## Section 18.1: Profiling Python Code

Profiling is the process of analyzing your code's runtime behavior to identify bottlenecks and performance issues. Python provides several built-in tools and third-party libraries for profiling your code. Let's explore some of the key concepts and tools related to profiling Python code.

### Why Profiling?

Profiling is essential because it helps you answer questions like:

- Which parts of your code are the slowest?
- Where is your code spending the most time?
- Are there memory issues like excessive memory consumption or memory leaks?

Profiling can reveal performance bottlenecks that might not be obvious through code inspection alone.

## Using cProfile

Python's standard library includes the cProfile module, which allows you to profile your code at the function level. Here's a simple example of how to use it:

```
import cProfile

def some_function():

# Your code here

if __name__ == "__main__":

cProfile.run("some_function()")
```

Running the script with cProfile will generate a report showing how much time is spent in each function and how many times they are called.

## Visualizing Profiling Data

To visualize profiling data, you can use external tools like snakeviz or the built-in pstats module. snakeviz generates interactive HTML reports, making it easier to identify performance issues.

## Line Profiling

In addition to function-level profiling, you can perform line-by-line profiling using tools like line_profiler. This allows you to pinpoint performance bottlenecks at a finer granularity.

## Memory Profiling

Memory profiling is essential for identifying memory-related issues, such as excessive memory consumption or memory leaks. The memory_profiler library is commonly used for this purpose. It shows memory usage for each line of code.

## Optimizing Based on Profiling Results

Once you've identified performance bottlenecks through profiling, you can focus on optimizing those specific parts of your code. This may involve algorithmic changes, data structure optimizations, or using external libraries and tools.

## Profiling Best Practices

- Profile real-world scenarios: Profile your code with realistic inputs and usage patterns to identify performance issues that users may encounter.

- Use context managers: When using external profiling tools, use context managers to start and stop profiling. This ensures that profiling is limited to the code you want to analyze.

- Profile before and after changes: Profiling should be an iterative process. Profile your code before making optimizations to establish a baseline, and then profile again after making changes to measure improvements.

Profiling is a valuable tool for optimizing Python code. By understanding where your code spends the most time and consumes memory, you can make targeted improvements to enhance the overall performance of your Python applications.

# Section 18.2: Optimizing CPU and Memory Usage

Optimizing CPU and memory usage is a crucial part of performance optimization in Python. In this section, we'll explore various techniques and best practices for reducing both CPU and memory usage in your Python programs.

## CPU Optimization Techniques

1. **Algorithmic Efficiency**: Choose efficient algorithms and data structures. The choice of the right algorithm can significantly reduce CPU usage. For example, using a set instead of a list for membership checks can lead to faster lookups.
2. **Avoid Global Variables**: Global variables can make your code harder to optimize. Minimize the use of global variables and prefer passing data as arguments to functions.
3. **List Comprehensions**: Use list comprehensions instead of for loops for constructing lists. List comprehensions are often faster and more readable.
4. **Generators**: When dealing with large datasets, use generators instead of lists to avoid loading the entire dataset into memory. Generators are memory-efficient and can reduce CPU usage.
5. **Caching**: Implement caching mechanisms for expensive function calls or data retrieval. Libraries like functools.lru_cache can help you cache results and avoid redundant computations.
6. **Parallelism**: Utilize multi-threading or multiprocessing to parallelize CPU-bound tasks. Python's concurrent.futures module simplifies parallelism and allows you to make better use of CPU cores.

7. **Profiling and Optimization**: Continuously profile your code to identify bottlenecks. Once bottlenecks are identified, apply targeted optimizations to those areas.

## Memory Optimization Techniques

1. **Avoid Unnecessary Data**: Remove unnecessary data structures or variables from memory when they are no longer needed. Use the del statement to delete references to objects.
2. **Generators**: As mentioned earlier, use generators for large datasets to avoid loading everything into memory at once. This can significantly reduce memory usage.
3. **Data Streaming**: Stream data instead of reading it all at once. For instance, use iterators to process large files line by line, rather than reading the entire file into memory.
4. **Memory Profiling**: Employ memory profiling tools like memory_profiler to identify memory-hungry parts of your code. Optimize or refactor these sections to reduce memory consumption.
5. **Data Compression**: If you're working with large volumes of data, consider using compression libraries like gzip or bz2 to reduce the memory footprint.
6. **Resource Management**: Explicitly release resources like file handles, database connections, and network sockets when they are no longer needed. Python's with statement is helpful for automatic resource cleanup.
7. **Data Serialization**: Choose efficient serialization formats like MessagePack or Protocol Buffers (as discussed in Chapter 9) to reduce the size of data when storing or transmitting it.
8. **Object Reuse**: Reuse objects instead of creating new ones, especially in loops. This can reduce memory allocation

overhead.

9. **Memory Views**: Use memory views (e.g., memoryview in Python) to avoid copying data when working with large arrays or buffers.
10. **Garbage Collection**: Python's garbage collector may not always release memory immediately. You can manually trigger garbage collection using gc.collect() when necessary.

Optimizing CPU and memory usage is an ongoing process, and the specific optimizations you apply will depend on your application's requirements and constraints. Profiling your code and using the appropriate tools and techniques are key to achieving optimal performance while minimizing resource usage in Python programs.

## Section 18.3: Cython and Just-In-Time Compilation

Cython is a superset of Python that allows you to write Python-like code with C-like performance. It achieves this by allowing you to add type annotations to Python code, which can then be compiled into C extensions. These C extensions can be imported and used in Python, providing significant speed improvements for CPU-bound tasks. In this section, we'll explore how to use Cython for optimizing CPU-bound Python code through just-in-time (JIT) compilation.

### Installing Cython

Before you can start using Cython, you need to install it. You can install Cython using pip:

```
pip install cython
```

Once Cython is installed, you're ready to optimize your Python code.

## Writing Cython Code

To use Cython, you'll need to create a .pyx file, which contains your Python-like code with type annotations. Here's a simple example:

```
# mymodule.pyx

def my_function(int x):

return x * 2
```

## Creating a setup.py Script

To compile your Cython code into a C extension, you need to create a setup.py script. Here's an example setup.py script:

```
from setuptools import setup

from Cython.Build import cythonize

setup(

ext_modules = cythonize("mymodule.pyx")

)
```

## Building the Extension

To build the Cython extension, run the following command in your terminal:

```
python setup.py build_ext—inplace
```

This command will generate a shared object file (.so on Unix-like systems) that you can import and use in your Python code.

## Using the Cython Extension

Once you've built the Cython extension, you can use it in your Python code like any other module:

```
# main.py

import mymodule

result = mymodule.my_function(42)

print(result)
```

## Profiling and Benchmarking

After using Cython to optimize your code, it's essential to profile and benchmark it to measure the performance improvements accurately. Python provides built-in profiling tools like cProfile, and you can also use external benchmarking libraries like timeit to compare the execution times before and after optimization.

Cython is a powerful tool for optimizing CPU-bound Python code, but it's worth noting that it may not provide significant performance improvements for all types of code. It's most effective when dealing with loops and operations that can benefit from low-level optimizations. Before using Cython, it's essential to identify the bottlenecks in your code and determine if Cython is the right tool for the job.

# Section 18.4: Parallel and Concurrent Programming

Parallel and concurrent programming are techniques used to improve the performance and responsiveness of Python applications by executing multiple tasks simultaneously. These techniques are particularly valuable for CPU-bound and I/O-bound tasks, allowing you to utilize multi-core processors and efficiently manage tasks that involve waiting for external resources. In this section, we'll explore parallelism and concurrency in Python.

## Parallel Programming

Parallel programming involves dividing a task into smaller sub-tasks that can be executed simultaneously on multiple CPU cores or processors. Python provides several libraries for parallel programming, including:

1. **Multiprocessing**: The multiprocessing module allows you to create multiple processes, each with its Python interpreter, and execute tasks in parallel. It's suitable for CPU-bound tasks.

```
import multiprocessing

def worker_function(x):

return x * 2

if __name__ == "__main__":

with multiprocessing.Pool(processes=4) as pool:

results = pool.map(worker_function, [1, 2, 3, 4, 5])

print(results)
```

1. **Thread-based Parallelism**: The threading module provides a way to create threads for parallel execution. However, due to Python's Global Interpreter Lock (GIL), threads may not provide significant performance

improvements for CPU-bound tasks. They are more suitable for I/O-bound tasks that involve waiting for external resources.

```
import threading

def worker_function(x):

return x * 2

threads = []

results = []

for i in range(4):

thread = threading.Thread(target=lambda x=i: results.append(worker_function(x)))

threads.append(thread)

thread.start()

for thread in threads:

thread.join()

print(results)
```

## Concurrent Programming

Concurrency involves managing multiple tasks that may run concurrently but not necessarily in parallel. Python provides several libraries and modules for concurrent programming:

1. **Asyncio**: The asyncio module allows you to write

asynchronous, non-blocking code using the async and await keywords. It's suitable for I/O-bound tasks that need to efficiently handle multiple simultaneous operations.

```
import asyncio

async def main():

tasks = [asyncio.create_task(worker_function(x)) for x in range(1, 6)]

results = await asyncio.gather(*tasks)

print(results)

asyncio.run(main())
```

1. **Threading**: As mentioned earlier, Python's threading module can be used for concurrent programming when dealing with I/O-bound tasks.
2. **Multiprocessing**: The multiprocessing module can also be used for concurrent execution when you need to run multiple processes concurrently.

Python's choice of parallel or concurrent programming techniques depends on the nature of the tasks you're dealing with. For CPU-bound tasks, parallelism with multiprocessing is a good choice, while I/O-bound tasks can benefit from concurrency using asyncio or threading. Properly using these techniques can lead to improved performance and responsiveness in your Python applications.

## Section 18.5: Performance Tuning Strategies

Performance tuning is a critical aspect of optimizing Python applications. It involves identifying and addressing bottlenecks and inefficiencies in your code to make it run faster and more efficiently. In this section, we'll explore various performance tuning strategies and best practices for Python applications.

## Profiling

Profiling is the process of measuring the execution time and resource usage of different parts of your code to identify performance bottlenecks. Python provides built-in tools and third-party libraries for profiling:

- **cProfile**: The cProfile module is a built-in profiler that can be used to measure the time spent in each function and the number of times they are called.

```
import cProfile

def my_function():

# Your code here

if __name__ == "__main__":

cProfile.run("my_function()")
```

- **line_profiler**: The line_profiler library allows you to profile individual lines of code, providing more granular insights into performance.

```
from line_profiler import LineProfiler

profiler = LineProfiler()

@profiler.profile
```

```
def my_function():

# Your code here

if __name__ == "__main__":

my_function()

profiler.print_stats()
```

## Optimizing CPU and Memory Usage

Optimizing CPU and memory usage is crucial for improving the overall performance of your Python applications. Here are some strategies:

- **Use Efficient Data Structures**: Choose the appropriate data structures for your tasks. Built-in data structures like lists, dictionaries, and sets are optimized for common use cases.

- **Avoid Global Variables**: Minimize the use of global variables, as they can slow down your code and make it harder to understand and maintain.

- **Memory Management**: Be mindful of memory usage, especially for large datasets. Use generators and iterators to process data lazily instead of loading everything into memory at once.

## Cython and Just-In-Time Compilation

Cython is a programming language that makes it easy to write C extensions for Python. By compiling your Python code with Cython, you can significantly improve its performance, especially for CPU-bound tasks.

Here's a simple example of using Cython to optimize a Python function:

```
# mymodule.pyx
def my_function(int n):
cdef int result = 0
for i in range(n):
result += i
return result
```

You can then compile this code using Cython:

```
cythonize -i mymodule.pyx
```

Now, you can use the optimized function in your Python code:

```
import mymodule
result = mymodule.my_function(1000000)
```

## Parallel and Concurrent Programming

As discussed earlier in this chapter, parallel and concurrent programming can significantly improve the performance of your Python applications by utilizing multiple CPU cores or handling multiple tasks simultaneously. Choose the appropriate technique based on your specific use case.

## Performance Tuning Tools

There are several third-party tools and libraries available for performance tuning and optimization in Python:

- **NumPy and SciPy**: When working with numerical and scientific computing, using optimized libraries like NumPy and SciPy can dramatically improve performance.

- **Numba**: Numba is a just-in-time (JIT) compiler for Python that can be used to speed up numerical computations.

- **PyPy**: PyPy is an alternative Python interpreter that employs a just-in-time compiler. It can often provide substantial performance improvements over the standard CPython interpreter.

## Continuous Monitoring and Testing

Performance tuning is an ongoing process. Regularly monitor and test your Python applications to ensure that they maintain optimal performance as your code evolves and data grows. Use benchmarks and profiling tools to identify performance regressions and address them promptly.

By following these performance tuning strategies and best practices, you can make your Python applications faster, more efficient, and better equipped to handle demanding workloads.

# Chapter 19: Web Development with Django

## Section 19.1: Introduction to Django

Django is a high-level Python web framework that encourages rapid development and clean, pragmatic design. It follows the "Don't Repeat Yourself" (DRY) and "Convention over Configuration" (CoC) principles, which means that developers can focus on writing their application's logic rather than dealing with repetitive tasks.

### Key Features of Django

Django comes with a rich set of features and components that simplify web development. Some of its key features include:

1. **Admin Interface**: Django provides an automatic admin interface for managing application data. Developers can define data models, and Django generates an admin interface for creating, updating, and deleting records.
2. **URL Routing**: Django's URL routing system allows developers to map URLs to views and functions easily. It helps create clean and organized URL structures for web applications.
3. **Template Engine**: Django has a powerful template engine that separates the HTML from Python code. This encourages the use of reusable templates and simplifies the front-end development process.
4. **ORM (Object-Relational Mapping)**: Django's ORM simplifies database interactions by allowing developers to work with Python objects instead of SQL queries. It supports multiple database backends.

5. **Authentication and Authorization**: Django provides built-in tools for user authentication and authorization. Developers can manage user accounts, permissions, and security features easily.
6. **Middleware**: Middleware components can be used to process requests and responses globally. This allows developers to implement cross-cutting concerns such as authentication, logging, and more.
7. **Security**: Django includes built-in protection against common web security vulnerabilities like SQL injection, cross-site scripting (XSS), and cross-site request forgery (CSRF).
8. **Internationalization and Localization**: Django supports multiple languages and provides tools for internationalization and localization of web applications.
9. **Testing**: Django encourages writing unit tests for applications. It provides a test framework for automating testing tasks.

## Django's Architecture

Django follows the Model-View-Controller (MVC) architectural pattern, although it refers to it as the Model-View-Template (MVT) pattern. Here's an overview of the components in Django's architecture:

- **Models**: Models define the structure and behavior of application data. They are represented as Python classes and map to database tables. Django's ORM handles database interactions.

- **Views**: Views are responsible for handling HTTP requests and returning HTTP responses. They contain the application's business logic.

- **Templates**: Templates are used for generating dynamic HTML content. They separate the presentation layer from the Python code in views.

- **URLs**: The URL dispatcher maps URLs to views. It defines the URL patterns for your web application.

- **Middleware**: Middleware components process requests and responses globally. They can perform tasks like authentication, logging, and more.

## Getting Started with Django

To start using Django, you'll need to install it, create a new Django project, and define your application's models, views, and templates. Here are the basic steps to get started:

1. Install Django using pip:

```
pip install Django
```

1. Create a new Django project:

```
django-admin startproject projectname
```

1. Create a new Django app within the project:

```
cd projectname

python manage.py startapp appname
```

1. Define your application's models in the app's models.py file, create database tables using migrations, and apply migrations:

```
python manage.py makemigrations

python manage.py migrate
```

1. Create views in the app's views.py file and define URL patterns in the project's urls.py file.
2. Create templates in the app's templates directory to render HTML content.
3. Start the development server:

```
python manage.py runserver
```

1. Access your web application in a web browser at http://localhost:8000/.

## Conclusion

Django is a powerful web framework for Python that simplifies web development tasks. In this section, we introduced Django's key features and architecture. To build web applications with Django, you'll need to understand its components, define models, views, and templates, and configure URL routing. Django's rich ecosystem of packages and its active community make it a popular choice for developing web applications of all sizes.

# Section 19.2: Building Web Applications with Django

In the previous section, we introduced Django and its key features. Now, let's delve deeper into building web applications with Django.

## Django Project Structure

When you create a new Django project using django-admin startproject projectname, it generates a directory structure that looks like this:

projectname/

manage.py

projectname/

__init__.py

settings.py

urls.py

asgi.py

wsgi.py

- manage.py: A command-line utility for managing various aspects of your project, such as running the development server, applying migrations, and creating apps.

- projectname/: This directory contains the actual Python package for your project.

– __init__.py: An empty file that tells Python that this directory should be considered a Python package.

– settings.py: Configuration settings for your project, including database settings, installed apps, and more.

– urls.py: URL patterns for your project. It maps URLs to views.

– asgi.py and wsgi.py: These files are used for ASGI and WSGI configurations, which are used to deploy your Django project to different servers.

## Creating Django Apps

In Django, a project can contain multiple apps. Each app is a self-contained module that can have its models, views, templates, and URL patterns. You can create a new app using the following command:

```
python manage.py startapp appname
```

This command generates a directory structure for the app, including a models.py file for defining data models, a views.py file for defining views, and a templates/ directory for HTML templates.

## Defining Models

Django's ORM makes it easy to define data models. Models are Python classes that map to database tables. You can define models in your app's models.py file. For example, here's a simple model for a blog post:

```
from django.db import models

class Post(models.Model):

title = models.CharField(max_length=200)

content = models.TextField()

pub_date = models.DateTimeField('date published')
```

Once you've defined your models, you can create database tables using migrations:

```
python manage.py makemigrations

python manage.py migrate
```

## Creating Views

Views in Django are Python functions or classes that handle HTTP requests and return HTTP responses. You define views in your app's views.py file. Here's a basic view that returns a list of blog posts:

```
from django.shortcuts import render

from .models import Post

def post_list(request):

posts = Post.objects.all()

return render(request, 'appname/post_list.html', {'posts': posts})
```

In this example, the post_list view retrieves all Post objects from the database and renders them using an HTML template.

## Templates

Django encourages the use of templates to separate the presentation layer from Python code. Templates are HTML files with placeholders for dynamic data. You can create templates in your app's templates/ directory and then render them in your views.

## URL Patterns

URL patterns in Django are defined in the urls.py files. You specify which view should handle each URL. Here's an example of defining a URL pattern for the post_list view:

```
from django.urls import path

from . import views

urlpatterns = [

path('posts/', views.post_list, name='post_list'),

]
```

Now, when you access http://localhost:8000/posts/, it will invoke the post_list view.

## Development Server

You can start the development server using the following command:

```
python manage.py runserver
```

This will run your Django application locally, and you can access it in a web browser at http://localhost:8000/.

## Conclusion

In this section, we explored the basics of building web applications with Django. We discussed the project structure, creating apps, defining models, creating views, working with templates, defining URL patterns, and running the development server. Django's well-defined structure and powerful features make it an excellent choice for web development projects of all sizes.

# Section 19.3: Working with Models, Views, and Templates in Django

In the previous section, we covered the basics of setting up a Django project and creating web applications. Now, let's dive deeper into working with models, views, and templates in Django.

## Models and the Database

Django's ORM (Object-Relational Mapping) allows you to define data models using Python classes. These models are then automatically translated into database tables. Let's extend our previous example of a blog post model:

```
from django.db import models

class Post(models.Model):

title = models.CharField(max_length=200)

content = models.TextField()

pub_date = models.DateTimeField('date published')

def __str__(self):

return self.title
```

In this updated model, we've added a __str__ method to provide a human-readable representation of each post. The pub_date field now includes a verbose_name to improve readability in the admin interface.

To create and apply migrations for the updated model, use the following commands:

```
python manage.py makemigrations
```

python manage.py migrate

## Django Admin Interface

Django comes with a powerful admin interface that allows you to manage your application's data. To enable the admin interface for your models, you need to register them. Create an admin.py file in your app directory and register your models:

```
from django.contrib import admin

from .models import Post

admin.site.register(Post)
```

Now, you can access the admin interface at http://localhost:8000/admin/ (assuming your development server is running). You can log in using the superuser account created earlier and manage your Post objects.

## Views and URL Patterns

Views in Django are responsible for processing HTTP requests and returning HTTP responses. We can create views to display lists of posts, individual post details, and more. Let's create a view to list all the blog posts:

```
from django.shortcuts import render

from .models import Post

def post_list(request):

posts = Post.objects.all()

return render(request, 'appname/post_list.html', {'posts': posts})
```

In this view, we retrieve all Post objects from the database and pass them to the post_list.html template.

To connect this view to a URL, define a URL pattern in your app's urls.py:

```
from django.urls import path

from . import views

urlpatterns = [

path('posts/', views.post_list, name='post_list'),

]
```

Now, when you access http://localhost:8000/appname/posts/, it will invoke the post_list view.

## Templates

Django encourages the use of templates to separate the presentation layer from your Python code. Templates are HTML files with placeholders for dynamic content. Create a templates directory in your app's directory and place your templates there. Here's a simplified example of a post_list.html template:

```
<!DOCTYPE html>

<html>

<head>

<title>Blog Post List</title>

</head>

<body>
```

```
<h1>Blog Posts</h1>

<ul>

{% for post in posts %}

<li><a href="{% url 'post_detail' post.id %}">{{ post.title }}</a></li>

{% endfor %}

</ul>

</body>

</html>
```

In this template, we use Django's template language to loop through the posts and display a list of blog post titles with links to their details.

## URL Patterns for Detail Views

To create a detail view for individual blog posts, we'll need to define a URL pattern and a corresponding view. In your app's urls.py, add the following:

```
urlpatterns = [

path('posts/', views.post_list, name='post_list'),

path('posts/<int:pk>/', views.post_detail, name='post_detail'),

]
```

Now, we have a URL pattern that captures the primary key (pk) of a post. In your views.py, create a post_detail view to handle these URLs and display the details of a single post.

## Conclusion

In this section, we explored how to work with models, views, and templates in Django. We defined data models, registered them in the admin interface, created views to handle HTTP requests, and used templates to render dynamic HTML content. Additionally, we set up URL patterns to map URLs to views, allowing users to interact with our web application. By following these Django conventions, you can efficiently develop robust web applications.

# Section 19.4: Authentication and Security in Django

In any web application, authentication and security are critical aspects to consider. Django provides built-in tools and best practices to help you handle user authentication, manage access control, and protect your application from common security vulnerabilities.

## User Authentication

Django's authentication system allows you to manage user accounts easily. To get started, make sure you have the django.contrib.auth app added to your project's INSTALLED_APPS in the settings.

### *User Registration*

To enable user registration, you can create a registration form using Django's forms framework. Here's a simplified example:

```
from django import forms

from django.contrib.auth.forms import UserCreationForm

from django.contrib.auth import login
```

```
from django.contrib.auth.models import User

class RegistrationForm(UserCreationForm):

email = forms.EmailField()

class Meta:

model = User

fields = ["username", "email", "password1", "password2"]

def register(request):

if request.method == "POST":

form = RegistrationForm(request.POST)

if form.is_valid():

user = form.save()

login(request, user)

# Redirect to a success page or dashboard

else:

form = RegistrationForm()

return render(request, "registration/register.html", {"form": form})
```

In this example, we create a RegistrationForm based on UserCreationForm but with an additional email field. Upon successful registration, the user is logged in, and you can redirect them to a dashboard or a success page.

*User Login and Logout*

Django provides built-in views and forms for user login and logout. You can include these views in your project's URLs and templates. Here's a simplified login view:

```
from django.contrib.auth import login, logout

from django.contrib.auth.forms import AuthenticationForm

def login_view(request):

if request.method == "POST":

form = AuthenticationForm(request, request.POST)

if form.is_valid():

user = form.get_user()

login(request, user)

# Redirect to a success page or dashboard

else:

form = AuthenticationForm()

return render(request, "registration/login.html", {"form": form})

def logout_view(request):

logout(request)

# Redirect to a logout success page
```

To include these views, add the following URL patterns to your app's urls.py:

```
from django.contrib.auth import views as auth_views

urlpatterns = [

path('login/', auth_views.LoginView.as_view(), name='login'),

path('logout/', auth_views.LogoutView.as_view(), name='logout'),

]
```

## Access Control and Permissions

Django provides a robust system for controlling access to views and objects. You can use decorators like @login_required to restrict access to authenticated users or @permission_required to restrict access to users with specific permissions. For example:

```
from django.contrib.auth.decorators import login_required, permission_required

@login_required

def protected_view(request):

# This view is accessible only to authenticated users

@permission_required('appname.change_modelname')

def change_model_view(request):

# This view requires 'change' permission on 'modelname'
```

## Security Best Practices

Django takes security seriously and provides built-in protection against common web vulnerabilities such as Cross-Site Scripting (XSS), Cross-Site Request Forgery (CSRF), and SQL injection. However, it's essential to follow best practices, including:

- Validating and sanitizing user input.
- Implementing proper session management.
- Using HTTPS for secure data transmission.
- Regularly updating Django and its dependencies to patch security vulnerabilities.
- Auditing and monitoring your application for security threats.

By following these best practices and utilizing Django's built-in security features, you can ensure that your web application remains secure and protects user data.

### Conclusion

Authentication and security are paramount in web development. Django simplifies the process by providing robust tools and conventions for user authentication, access control, and protection against common security threats. By following Django's best practices and keeping security considerations in mind, you can build secure web applications with confidence.

## Section 19.5: Deploying Django Applications

Once you've developed a Django web application, the next step is to deploy it to a production server so that it's accessible to users on the internet. Deploying a Django application involves several steps, including setting up a production environment, configuring the web server, and ensuring proper security and performance. In this section, we'll explore the key considerations and steps for deploying a Django application.

## 1. Choose a Hosting Provider

Before you can deploy your Django application, you need to choose a hosting provider or server where your application will run. Some popular options for hosting Django applications include:

- **Platform as a Service (PaaS) Providers:** Services like Heroku, PythonAnywhere, and Google App Engine offer easy deployment options for Django applications, with built-in scalability and management.

- **Virtual Private Servers (VPS):** Providers like AWS, DigitalOcean, and Linode offer VPS hosting, giving you full control over your server's configuration and scalability.

- **Dedicated Servers:** For larger applications, dedicated servers from providers like AWS, Google Cloud, and others allow maximum customization and control.

- **Containerized Deployments:** You can use containerization platforms like Docker and orchestration tools like Kubernetes to deploy and manage Django applications in containers.

Choose a hosting option that aligns with your application's requirements, budget, and your level of expertise.

## 2. Set Up a Production Environment

Configuring a production environment involves several steps, including:

- **Installing Required Software:** Ensure that your server has Python, a web server (e.g., Nginx or Apache), and a database server (e.g., PostgreSQL or MySQL) installed.

- **Setting Up a Virtual Environment:** Create a virtual environment to isolate your application's dependencies.

- **Configuring Environment Variables:** Use environment variables to store sensitive information like database credentials and secret keys securely.

- **Collecting Static Files:** In production, you'll need to collect static files using collectstatic to serve them efficiently.

## 3. Configure Web Server and Database

Configure your web server (e.g., Nginx or Apache) to serve your Django application using WSGI (Web Server Gateway Interface). Connect your Django application to the production database (e.g., PostgreSQL or MySQL) and set up database configurations in your Django settings.

## 4. Secure Your Application

Security is critical in production. Implement security best practices, including:

- Enabling HTTPS with an SSL certificate.

- Using strong, unique passwords and secret keys.

- Applying security patches regularly.

- Implementing proper authentication and authorization.

- Configuring firewalls and security groups.

## 5. Set Up Deployment Scripts

Create deployment scripts or use automation tools (e.g., Fabric or Ansible) to streamline the deployment process. These scripts should automate tasks like code deployment, database migrations, and server configuration.

## 6. Monitor and Maintain

After deploying your Django application, regularly monitor server performance, log files, and error reports. Implement error tracking and performance monitoring tools to detect and address issues promptly.

## 7. Scaling

As your application grows, consider strategies for scaling, such as load balancing, caching, and horizontal scaling by adding more servers.

## Conclusion

Deploying a Django application to production involves careful planning and configuration. Choose the right hosting provider, set up a production environment, configure the web server and database, prioritize security, automate deployment processes, monitor your application, and be prepared to scale as needed. Following these steps will help you deploy a robust and reliable Django web application for your users to enjoy.

# Chapter 20: Flask: Creating Web APIs

## Section 20.1: Introduction to Flask

Flask is a lightweight and versatile micro web framework for Python. It is designed to make it easy to build web applications and RESTful APIs quickly with minimal boilerplate code. Flask follows the WSGI (Web Server Gateway Interface) specification and is a great choice for developers who want a simple yet powerful toolset for web development.

### Key Features of Flask:

1. **Minimalistic:** Flask is minimalistic and unopinionated, which means it doesn't impose strict rules on how you should structure your application. You have the freedom to choose the components and libraries that best suit your project.
2. **Built-in Development Server:** Flask comes with a built-in development server that makes it easy to test your application during development.
3. **Jinja2 Templates:** Flask integrates seamlessly with the Jinja2 templating engine, allowing you to create dynamic HTML templates for your web pages.
4. **RESTful Support:** Flask is well-suited for building RESTful APIs, making it a popular choice for backend development in combination with frontend frameworks like React, Angular, or Vue.js.
5. **Extension Ecosystem:** Flask has a rich ecosystem of extensions that can be added to your application as needed. These extensions cover a wide range of functionalities, from database integration to authentication and

authorization.

## Getting Started with Flask:

To start using Flask, you'll need to install it. You can install Flask using pip, Python's package manager, with the following command:

```
pip install Flask
```

Once Flask is installed, you can create a simple "Hello, World!" application to get a feel for how it works:

```
from flask import Flask

app = Flask(__name__)

@app.route('/')

def hello_world():

return 'Hello, World!'

if __name__ == '__main__':

app.run()
```

In this example:

- We import the Flask class from the flask module.
- We create a Flask web application instance.
- We define a route using the @app.route() decorator. In this case, the route is the root URL ('/').
- We define a function, hello_world(), that is executed when a user accesses the root URL. This function returns 'Hello, World!' as the response.

- Finally, we start the Flask development server with app.run().

You can run this script, and your Flask application will be accessible at http://localhost:5000/. This is a basic introduction to Flask, and we will explore more advanced topics in subsequent sections, including routing, templates, database integration, and creating RESTful APIs.

## Section 20.2: Building RESTful APIs with Flask

Flask's simplicity and flexibility make it an excellent choice for building RESTful APIs (Application Programming Interfaces). RESTful APIs are a way to expose your application's functionality to other systems or developers over the internet. In this section, we'll explore how to create RESTful APIs using Flask.

### Creating a Basic RESTful API

To create a basic RESTful API with Flask, you need to define routes that correspond to different API endpoints (e.g., /api/users, /api/products). Each endpoint typically maps to a specific resource or functionality.

Here's an example of creating a simple RESTful API that manages a list of tasks:

```
from flask import Flask, request, jsonify

app = Flask(__name__)

tasks = []

@app.route('/api/tasks', methods=['GET'])
```

```
def get_tasks():
return jsonify({'tasks': tasks})
@app.route('/api/tasks', methods=['POST'])
def create_task():
data = request.get_json()
task = {'id': len(tasks) + 1, 'title': data['title']}
tasks.append(task)
return jsonify({'message': 'Task created successfully'}), 201
if __name__ == '__main__':
app.run()
```

In this example:

- We define a Flask application and create an empty list called tasks to store our task data.
- We create two routes:

  – GET /api/tasks: This route returns a JSON representation of all tasks when accessed.

  – POST /api/tasks: This route allows you to create a new task by sending a JSON payload with a 'title' field in the request body.

You can test this API using a tool like curl[1] or Postman[2]. For instance, you can create a new task using the following curl command:

1. https://curl.se/

curl -X POST -H "Content-Type: application/json" -d '{"title": "Buy groceries"}' http://localhost:5000/api/tasks

## Handling Request Data

Flask provides the request object to access data from incoming requests. In the example above, we used request.get_json() to parse JSON data from the request body. Flask supports various methods for retrieving data, such as request.args for query parameters and request.form for form data.

## HTTP Methods and Status Codes

RESTful APIs adhere to HTTP methods like GET, POST, PUT, DELETE, etc., and use appropriate status codes to indicate the success or failure of requests. In our example, we used methods=['GET'] and methods=['POST'] to specify which HTTP methods are allowed for each route. We also returned status code 201 (Created) when a new task is created successfully.

This basic example demonstrates the foundation of building RESTful APIs with Flask. In practice, you'll often work with more complex data, authentication, and error handling. Flask extensions like Flask-RESTful and Flask-RESTPlus can help you streamline API development by providing tools and abstractions for common tasks.

# Section 20.3: Authentication and Authorization

Authentication and authorization are crucial aspects of building secure web APIs with Flask. Authentication verifies the identity of users or systems, while authorization determines what actions they

2. https://www.postman.com/

are allowed to perform once authenticated. In this section, we'll explore how to implement these security measures in your Flask-based web API.

## Implementing Authentication

There are various methods to implement authentication in a Flask web API, but one of the most common approaches is using JSON Web Tokens (JWT). JWTs are compact and self-contained tokens that can be used to authenticate users or systems.

To get started, you'll need to install the necessary packages, including Flask-JWT-Extended:

```
pip install Flask-JWT-Extended
```

Here's a basic example of how to implement JWT-based authentication in Flask:

```
from flask import Flask, jsonify, request

from flask_jwt_extended import JWTManager, create_access_token, jwt_required, get_jwt_identity

app = Flask(__name__)

app.config['JWT_SECRET_KEY'] = 'your-secret-key' # Change this to a strong, secret key

jwt = JWTManager(app)

users = {'user1': 'password1', 'user2': 'password2'}

@app.route('/api/login', methods=['POST'])

def login():
```

```
data = request.get_json()
username = data['username']
password = data['password']
if username in users and users[username] == password:
access_token = create_access_token(identity=username)
return jsonify({'access_token': access_token}), 200
else:
return jsonify({'message': 'Invalid credentials'}), 401
@app.route('/api/protected', methods=['GET'])
@jwt_required()
def protected():
current_user = get_jwt_identity()
return jsonify({'message': f'Hello, {current_user}! This is a protected resource.'}), 200
if __name__ == '__main__':
app.run()
```

In this example:

- We use Flask-JWT-Extended to handle JWT-based authentication. You can set your secret key in the JWT_SECRET_KEY configuration variable.

• We define a login route that accepts a POST request with a username and password in the request body. If the credentials are valid, it returns a JWT access token.

• We create a protected route that requires authentication using the @jwt_required() decorator. Only users with a valid JWT can access this route.

To test this authentication flow, you can use a tool like Postman[3] or curl[4]. First, obtain a token by sending a POST request to /api/login with valid credentials. Then, include the token in the Authorization header (e.g., Bearer <token>) when accessing protected routes.

## Implementing Authorization

Authorization determines what authenticated users are allowed to do. It's typically done by associating roles or permissions with users and checking those roles or permissions when a user attempts an action.

Flask-Principal is a helpful extension for managing roles and permissions in Flask applications. You can install it using pip:

pip install Flask-Principal

Here's a simple example of implementing authorization with Flask-Principal:

**from** flask **import** Flask, jsonify

**from** flask_principal **import** Principal, Permission

app = Flask(__name__)

3. https://www.postman.com/

4. https://curl.se/

```
principal = Principal(app)

admin_permission = Permission()

@app.route('/api/admin', methods=['GET'])

@admin_permission.require(http_exception=403)

def admin():

return jsonify({'message': 'Welcome, admin! You have access to this resource.'}), 200

if __name__ == '__main__':

app.run()
```

In this example:

- We import Flask-Principal and create a Principal object for our app.
- We define an admin_permission using Permission().
- The /api/admin route is protected with the @admin_permission.require(http_exception=403) decorator. This decorator ensures that only users with the admin_permission can access the route.

You can extend this by associating roles or permissions with users and checking them in your route handlers.

These examples provide a foundation for implementing authentication and authorization in your Flask-based web APIs. Depending on your application's complexity, you may need to explore more advanced security mechanisms and integrate with identity providers like OAuth or OpenID Connect for user authentication.

# Section 20.4: Testing and Documentation

Testing and documentation are essential aspects of creating robust and maintainable Flask web APIs. In this section, we'll explore how to write tests for your Flask application and how to document your API to make it accessible to other developers.

## Writing Tests with Flask-Testing

Testing your Flask application ensures that it functions correctly and helps catch bugs early in the development process. Flask-Testing is a popular extension for writing unit tests and integration tests for Flask applications. You can install it using pip:

```
pip install Flask-Testing
```

Here's an example of how to write tests for a Flask application:

```
import unittest

from flask import Flask

from flask_testing import TestCase

app = Flask(__name__)

app.config['TESTING'] = True

class MyTest(TestCase):

def create_app(self):

return app
```

```
def test_index(self):

response = self.client.get('/')

self.assertEqual(response.status_code, 200)

self.assertIn(b'Hello, World!', response.data)

if __name__ == '__main__':

unittest.main()
```

In this example:

- We create a Flask application and set the TESTING configuration to True.
- We define a test class that inherits from TestCase.
- Inside the test class, we define a test method (test_index) that sends a GET request to the / route and asserts that the response status code is 200 and that the response data contains "Hello, World!".

You can run the tests using the unittest.main() method. Writing tests like these helps ensure that your API endpoints work as expected and allows for automated testing as you continue to develop your application.

## Documenting Your Flask API

Documentation is crucial for making your Flask API accessible and understandable to other developers, including those who may want to consume your API. One popular tool for creating API documentation is Swagger, which allows you to generate interactive API documentation.

To generate Swagger documentation for your Flask API, you can use the flask-restplus extension, which builds on top of Flask-RESTful and integrates with Swagger. Install it using pip:

```
pip install flask-restplus
```

Here's an example of how to use Flask-RESTPlus for API documentation:

```
from flask import Flask

from flask_restplus import Api, Resource

app = Flask(__name__)

api = Api(app, version='1.0', title='My API', description='An example API')

@api.route('/hello')

class HelloResource(Resource):

def get(self):

"""Returns a friendly greeting."""

return {'message': 'Hello, World!'}

if __name__ == '__main__':

app.run()
```

In this example:

- We create a Flask application and initialize Flask-RESTPlus with API information such as version, title, and description.

- We define a resource (HelloResource) that represents an API endpoint.

- Inside the resource, we use docstrings to provide documentation for the endpoint. The docstring for the get method describes what the endpoint does.

To access the Swagger documentation, run your Flask application and navigate to http://localhost:5000/api/. You'll find interactive documentation that allows users to explore and test your API.

In summary, testing and documentation are essential parts of building a Flask web API. Writing tests ensures the reliability of your application, while proper documentation makes it accessible and understandable to other developers and users. Consider using tools like Flask-Testing and Flask-RESTPlus to streamline these processes.

## Section 20.5: Deploying Flask APIs

Deploying a Flask API is the final step in making it accessible to users on the internet. In this section, we'll explore various deployment options and best practices for deploying Flask APIs.

### Deployment Options

There are several ways to deploy a Flask API, depending on your requirements and expertise. Here are some common deployment options:

#### *1. Cloud Platforms*

Cloud platforms like Amazon Web Services (AWS), Google Cloud Platform (GCP), and Microsoft Azure offer scalable infrastructure for hosting Flask APIs. You can deploy your API as a web application on a virtual machine (VM) or use serverless platforms like AWS Lambda or Google Cloud Functions.

*2. Platform-as-a-Service (PaaS)*

PaaS providers like Heroku and PythonAnywhere simplify the deployment process. You can deploy your Flask API by pushing your code to a Git repository, and the PaaS platform handles server provisioning and configuration.

*3. Docker Containers*

Using Docker, you can package your Flask application and its dependencies into a container image. You can then deploy this container image to container orchestration platforms like Kubernetes or Docker Swarm.

*4. Traditional Web Hosting*

You can deploy a Flask API on traditional web hosting platforms that provide server access. This typically involves configuring a web server (e.g., Apache or Nginx) to serve your Flask application using a web server gateway interface (WSGI) server like Gunicorn or uWSGI.

## Best Practices for Deployment

Regardless of the deployment option you choose, here are some best practices to follow when deploying Flask APIs:

*1. Use Environment Variables*

Avoid hardcoding sensitive information like API keys, database URLs, and secret keys in your code. Instead, use environment variables to store such configurations. Tools like python-decouple[5] or python-dotenv[6] can help manage environment variables.

*2. Secure Your API*

Implement security best practices such as HTTPS, authentication, and authorization. Use tools like Flask-Security[7] to handle user authentication and authorization.

*3. Configure Logging*

Set up logging to capture errors and events in your Flask application. Logging helps you troubleshoot issues in production. The Python logging module is a standard choice for logging.

*4. Monitor and Scale*

Implement monitoring and alerting to keep an eye on your API's performance. Services like Amazon CloudWatch, Google Cloud Monitoring, or third-party tools like Prometheus can help. Be prepared to scale your application horizontally when traffic increases.

---

5. https://pypi.org/project/python-decouple/
6. https://pypi.org/project/python-dotenv/
7. https://flask-security-too.readthedocs.io/en/stable/

***5. Backup and Disaster Recovery***

Regularly back up your data and codebase. Have a disaster recovery plan in place in case of server failures or data corruption. Services like AWS S3 or Azure Blob Storage are suitable for data backup.

***6. Continuous Integration and Deployment (CI/CD)***

Set up a CI/CD pipeline to automate the testing and deployment of your Flask API. Tools like Jenkins, Travis CI, or GitLab CI/CD can help streamline this process.

***7. Documentation***

Maintain clear and up-to-date documentation for your API. Tools like Swagger or ReDoc can generate interactive API documentation.

***8. Versioning***

Consider implementing API versioning to ensure backward compatibility as your API evolves. This can be done by including the version number in the API URL or using custom headers.

***9. Application Performance***

Optimize your Flask API for performance. Techniques like caching, database indexing, and code profiling can help improve response times.

*10. Regular Updates and Security Patching*

Keep your dependencies and server software up to date. Regularly apply security patches to protect your API from known vulnerabilities.

In conclusion, deploying a Flask API involves selecting an appropriate deployment option and following best practices to ensure security, scalability, and maintainability. Consider your project's requirements and choose the deployment strategy that best fits your needs.

www.ingramcontent.com/pod-product-compliance
Lightning Source LLC
LaVergne TN
LVHW090304210926
848480LV00001B/128